# PATRIOT ACTS

## WHAT AMERICANS MUST DO TO SAVE THE REPUBLIC

## Catherine Crier

Threshold Editions
New York   London   Toronto   Sydney   New Delhi

Threshold Editions
A Division of Simon & Schuster, Inc.
1230 Avenue of the Americas
New York, NY 10020

Copyright © 2011 by Catherine Crier

First Threshold Editions hardcover edition November 2011

THRESHOLD EDITIONS and colophon are trademarks of Simon & Schuster, Inc.

For information about special discounts for bulk purchases,
please contact Simon & Schuster Special Sales at 1-866-506-1949
or business@simonandschuster.com.

The Simon & Schuster Speakers Bureau can bring authors to your live event.
For more information or to book an event contact the Simon & Schuster Speakers Bureau
at 1-866-248-3049 or visit our website at www.simonspeakers.com.

Designed by Renata Di Biase

Manufactured in the United States of America

10   9   8   7   6   5   4   3   2   1

Library of Congress Cataloging-in-Publication Data is available.

ISBN 978-1-4391-9543-7
ISBN 978-1-4391-9494-2 (ebook)

Cartoon on page 4 © 2011 Gahan Wilson, published by Fantagraphics Books

*To the Founders, some idealists,*
*others more pragmatic, but revolutionaries all,*
*who believed that a more perfect union was possible.*
*And to all patriots who struggle to make their dream a reality.*

# CONTENTS

Dear Reader,

I am an American by birth, but my intense passion for this country is a product of so much more. As long as I can remember, I have been fascinated by the origins and evolution of our Republic. From grade school through college, I studied American history, politics, and international affairs: from the insurgent movement that sparked a revolution and the great debates that shaped our founding documents, through the myriad ways our constitutional system has been interpreted and applied by politicians, judges, and the people themselves. As a law student, then an attorney and judge, I focused on the impact of our legal system—who makes the rules and why, how they are applied or abused, and whether they enhance or diminish our lives and national values. For the last twenty-two years, I have worked as a journalist, investigating and reporting on events in real time and interviewing and debating key players—government leaders, generals, CEOs, political activists, and regular citizens.

In this book, I examine what the Framers intended, how their vision has been interpreted over time, and how resulting policies and laws shape the nation. How do our modern parties compare to their predecessors? What do they pitch on the campaign trail, and how do they actually govern? What are the results, and what is the impact on American citizens and the nation as a whole? Most important, how do these outcomes stack up with our founding principles? I discuss how and why we've arrived at this moment in history and what we must do to realign ourselves with the remarkable vision entrusted to this generation.

As you continue reading, try a little experiment. Set aside any assumptions and ideologies and consider each issue through the eyes of an American patriot. For it was with such a heart and mind that I wrote these words.

# PATRIOT
# ACTS

# INTRODUCTION

If a house be divided against itself, that house cannot stand.

*—Abraham Lincoln, quoting Mark's gospel*

I am afraid for my country. America has weathered disasters before, but today, the confluence of national and international crises has created a perfect storm of fear and unrest. Financial devastation, social and cultural upheaval, a decade of war, homegrown terrorism, environmental disruption—the range, magnitude, and complexity of these problems is unprecedented. The tangible impact on our lives is enormous, but so is the toll on our national psyche.

For generations, the American Dream has been within reach for most citizens. Not everyone would grab the brass ring, but we all had a shot. With hard work, perseverance, and just a bit of luck, most people could join the middle class, buy a home, educate their kids, and expect a modicum of security as they aged. That promise has been fading for quite some time, but as a nation, we are wonderfully, stubbornly optimistic and have kept the faith. Suddenly, it vanished, and millions of people want to know why. Why, through no fault of their own, are they out on the street or out of a job while U.S. corporate profits reach their highest levels since 1988? Why are their kids failing in school? Why is the nation drowning

Republicans in the Wisconsin statehouse didn't need guns to overthrow our political system. Deciding that their majority status trumped legislative rules, in 2011, they voted to eliminate collective bargaining in that state without a quorum present. So what if the Democrats weren't even in the building? Then, they authorized the new GOP governor, Scott Walker, to disband local elected governments and appoint a private overseer to manage cities and towns if he alone deemed it an economic necessity. These are the actions of a dictator and puppet government, not those of elected officials in a constitutional republic.

As I watch the political battles escalate, I am reminded of an old Gahan Wilson cartoon. An infantryman stands alone in a barren, smoldering landscape. Absolutely nothing is left alive. The punch line: "I think I won!"

*"I think I won!"*

Convinced that the mission is just and true, many hard-liners do not understand that their vision, if realized, would destroy what they claim to defend. This land would remain, and the victors could lay claim to it, but its heart and soul, the greatness that is America, would be gone.

There is a real battle to be joined in this country, just not the one so many are waging. When rhetoric and ideological warfare threaten the very pillars of our democracy, true patriots must act. They must do so armed with facts, not myths, and with a real understanding of the extraordinary but fragile system our Founders established.

At the close of the Constitutional Convention, Benjamin Franklin was asked, "What sort of government have we?" He replied, "A Republic, if you can keep it." It is time we rally in its defense.

# *What Sort of Government Have We?*

Americans love our country deeply, and when told we're losing it, nothing can stop us from fighting. But there seems to be a lot of confusion these days about the mission. What exactly did the Founders establish? What is now at risk, and what must be done to preserve the Republic?

Our Founders created a constitutional government that would protect and promote a free and diverse society. This secular system was based on the emerging political philosophy known as "classical liberalism," which advocated individual liberty, private property, and representative democracy. This philosophy was shared by the American revolutionaries, conservatives and liberals alike. During the drafting and debates, vigorous attempts were made to skew the Constitution left or right, but they were defeated. Those who argue otherwise are misleading you intentionally or are ignorant of historical facts.

In 1789, when these men gathered in Philadelphia to draft the Constitution, two groups fought vigorously to dominate the convention. Conservatives wanted another England. Alexander Hamilton argued for a monarch and a House of Lords. They believed in a strong central government ruled by the elite. The liberals feared control by an American aristocracy. They were quite radical in their struggle to limit such power. Benjamin Franklin wanted a single

House of Representatives with members elected every year and argued against the presidency, preferring an executive council. The conservatives sought economic growth and civil order. The liberals wanted individual liberty and real assurance that average citizens would have a strong voice in the nation's affairs. Each side believed passionately in the righteousness of its position and greatly mistrusted the opposition.

The Constitution that emerged from this convention became known as James Madison's Grand Compromise, a triumph of visionary wisdom over partisan self-interest. Neither the conservatives nor the liberals gave up their beliefs about the best way to lead the nation. What they abandoned was the chance to rig the game, and in return, they accepted a neutral playing field and the chance to compete fairly in the marketplace of ideas. Their political theories would be tested in the public arena and would face a referendum at the ballot box every two, four, or six years. Win or lose, power would transfer peacefully, and the work of governing would continue. If unhappy with the results, citizens could change course in the next election.

To call this system neutral is not quite accurate: Actually, it promoted competition by design. Knowing the dangers of direct democracy and how quickly an impassioned majority can impose its will, both conservatives and liberals wanted a representative democracy. But even an elected majority would be constrained by our Constitution and Bill of Rights. These documents create multiple checks and balances across three branches of government, including presidential vetoes, congressional overrides, a complex amendment process, and independent judicial review, all designed to temper power and ensure that minority voices would be heard. Interestingly, the wealthy conservatives were adamant about this. Already outnumbered, they feared that Thomas Jefferson's common man, the general population, might seek to suppress their interests.

On the day our Constitution was adopted, Franklin addressed the Convention, saying, "If every one of us in returning to our constituents were to report the objections he has had to it . . . we might prevent its being generally received and thereby lose all."[1] But the Framers realized that the whole was greater than the sum of its parts, and their crowning achievement was to make a vigorous democratic process, not partisan ideology, our constitutional mandate.

Our first political parties emerged before the ink was dry on this noble document, and the race was on to reframe its mandate and institutionalize partisan advantage. That our system survives, relatively intact, is a testament to the power of our democratic ideals and the willingness of the American people, generation after generation, to defend them above special interests and partisan beliefs. Without the push-pull of ideas between liberals and conservatives, our nation would be a very different place, one I suggest neither side would like. Unchecked conservatism becomes authoritarian and tyrannical, allowing a small group of the powerful elite to govern with few checks on their actions. Extreme liberalism moves toward socialism, even communism, and delivers control to a different group, government bureaucrats, but still arrives at the same place—tyranny. Pure liberty leads to anarchy, and guess what that vacuum invites? Might makes right, and that equals tyranny.

Political parties attract like minds, and from their earliest moments, our conservative and liberal factions have exhibited rather consistent personalities. My point about the need for balance is made clear if you imagine what happens if a somewhat controlling, authoritarian father has no counterbalance in the mother. He may help a scattered family focus on specific goals but fail to see the drawbacks to his single-mindedness. He will act quickly when threatened, but he can go off half-cocked, refusing to take much-needed advice. Confident that his views are the right ones, he doesn't tolerate debate or dissent, preferring that his wards march to a single tune. To him, securing the family is more important than promoting the community's welfare, so in troubled times, he will grab up resources, leaving others to fend for themselves. The mother seeks to balance interests. She cannot be narrowly focused, as the long-term well-being of the family is her goal. She wants each member to be happy and tolerates their unique choices, loving them no matter what. She sees that a healthy community makes her own kids safer when they venture out, so she expands her mission beyond the family circle. But at times, she might listen too long to competing voices and try too hard to make everyone happy. Important missions might be neglected as she tolerates too much input or chaotic behavior. This is, of course, a gross simplification, but at their core, conservatives seek order and liberals pursue freedom. Maintaining a balance produces the healthiest, most productive results over the long run.

Conservative icon Friedrich A. von Hayek was lauded by Ronald Reagan and Margaret Thatcher as one of the intellectuals most responsible for their own political philosophies. His most recognized work is likely *The Road to Serfdom*. One article they may have missed is entitled *Why I Am Not a Conservative*. In it, he discusses how political philosophy and personality coincide and the dangers this presents to a real democracy.

Hayek could not come up with a name for his own political philosophy. Writing in 1960 and knowing that the terms "liberal" and "progressive" had been hijacked from their classical meaning, he wasn't sure what to call himself. But he adamantly rejected the conservative label for several reasons. His observations, objections, and descriptions of what he believed were true American principles are right on target today.

Hayek applauded the Founders' "courage and confidence, [their] preparedness to let change run its course even if we cannot predict where it will lead." Our first political leaders were progressives in the true sense of the word—designing a future, not clinging to the past. He was frustrated that modern conservatives defend an imaginary status quo despite the inevitability of change. He objected to their tendency to put the brakes on progress without offering a different course. "The tug of war between conservatives and progressives can only affect the speed, not the direction, of contemporary developments. The critical question for any American is not how fast or how far we should move, *but where we should move*, for move we will."

Hayek noted similarities between modern conservatives and socialists (not liberals): Both groups are content to expand government as long as they are in control. "The conservative does not object to coercion or arbitrary power so long as it is used for what he regards as the right purposes. He believes that if government is in the hands of decent men, it ought not to be too much restricted by rigid rules . . . he is less concerned with the problem of how the powers of government should be limited than with that of who wields them . . . like the socialist, he regards himself as entitled to force the values he holds on other people."

While possessed of strong moral principles, he found that many conservatives do not hold strong *democratic* convictions. Our system requires healthy debate, willingness to work with political opponents, and respect for our system of government even when that system thwarts certain conservative objectives. Every American should defend theses principles above partisan advantage.

These comments by Hayek were not addressing policy issues— what sort of taxes or regulations we should have or whether an international crisis calls for military intervention. Instead, he was talking about the tendency of conservatives to challenge or ignore our most fundamental constitutional principles when they block certain goals or permit outcomes the group opposes.

Hayek said, "I believe that the conservatives deceive themselves when they blame the evils of our time on democracy. The chief evil is unlimited government, and nobody is qualified to wield unlimited power." That power could reside in an overreaching bureaucracy, or, even worse, might be handed to a single president by congressional decree. Hayek concluded that "it is not who governs but what government is entitled to do that seems to me the essential problem."

He did not address the pros or cons of American liberals; but notably, socialists were his counterpoint to conservatives—the progressives were somewhere in the middle. His criticisms were targeted, but the observations create an essential checklist for a healthy democracy.

In recent years, the partisan attack on our system of government has been relentless. After 9/11, the Bush administration took actions that far exceeded executive authority, building what is now known as a "unitary presidency." Throughout Bush's tenure, the Republican-led Congress and Department of Justice served as a rubber stamp, willingly abdicating their power to the executive branch as Americans were spied on, civil and legal rights were curtailed, and martial law was expanded, to list just a few of the questionable, even unconstitutional measures of that time.

There is nothing patriotic about granting such powers to leaders simply because we agree with their positions. There is nothing American about abusing the rule of law or ignoring the Constitution when "our side" is in control. Just as FDR's Democratic Congress would not let him pack the Supreme Court, and the Republican Party led the push for Nixon's resignation, true patriots will oppose actions by either party that seek to thwart the democratic process or secure power that exceeds constitutional authority.

Today, many conservatives claim that President Obama is overreaching on health care or stimulus spending, while liberals say the same about his use of military and security powers. If these claims are true, both sides should look in the mirror for the real culprits. Congress cannot claim surprise when succeeding administrations use the power it gave up when it was politically expedient to do so.

International threats and tough economic times always increase social tensions, and the call to restrict freedoms is a predictable response. The battle is twofold; the curtailing of our liberty in the name of security is one concern, but so is the targeting of particular groups within our population. Virtually every ethnic and racial group—the French, Irish, Chinese, Japanese, African Americans and others—has been demonized at some point in our history. Most of us would laugh at the notion that a Catholic president might turn over our government to the pope, yet this was a serious concern when John F. Kennedy campaigned in 1960. Today, Hispanics and Muslims are in the crosshairs.

A dramatic shift in our demographics is underway, with Hispanics on target to become a majority in the United States by 2050, and illegal immigration is a major economic and security issue. Since 9/11, global terrorism has dominated our foreign policy, and now, incidents have sparked concern over the rise of homegrown terrorists inspired by Islamic fundamentalists. These issues should be at the top of our political agenda, but the *manner* in which they are being addressed is of great concern.

Many politicians play on our fear and anger to score points with their base, while certain commentators do it for ratings, promoting draconian measures and severe crackdowns to demonstrate they are tough on these problems. The prospect of gutting our constitutional protections does not disturb them. Nor is truth an obstacle, as they weave fantastic renderings of our history and produce data from thin air to justify their positions.

A fair number of Republicans now believe that President

Obama is a Muslim (he is not), and conservative state legislatures across the country are scrambling to stop an imagined spread of Sharia law. In March 2011, Republican Congressman Peter King launched hearings to investigate the nation's entire Muslim American community based on its Islamic faith, rejecting efforts to limit his inquiry to radical elements that might actually threaten our security.

Glenn Beck told his Fox News viewers that radical fundamentalists were behind the democratic uprisings in the Middle East and then made extraordinary leaps to tie terrorists to the American left, claiming that our unions are in cahoots with Egyptian radicals. On air, Beck professes to be a student of history and politics as he manufactures evidence to justify outrageous theories and proposals. Yet when interviewed in *Forbes* magazine in April 2010, Beck was surprisingly candid, saying, "I could give a flying crap about the political process. We're an entertainment company." Sadly, many followers, including some Republican officeholders, recite his imaginings as truth. Meanwhile, Beck is laughing all the way to the bank.

It has taken several years for thoughtful conservatives to realize just how destructive a small group of reactionary pundits and politicians can be to their party. It's the old adage about riding the tiger—sooner or later, you're going to get eaten. By the spring of 2011, George Will and other respected voices on the right began challenging the credentials of people like Beck, Michele Bachmann, and Sarah Palin as they realized the damage these people were doing to true conservatism and to our constitutional system of government.

I am all for those who challenge entrenched interests on their own side of the aisle while vigorously debating the political opposition. Both political parties are failing the American people and need strong members to shake things up. I do not agree with some of Congressman Ron Paul's positions, but he uses intelligent, reasoned arguments to defend even unconventional proposals. He has no problem taking on his Republican leaders or challenging entrenched interests that ignore the needs of the American people. His is an important voice in our political debate. But when mavericks choose the easy path—divisive rhetoric, historical falsehoods, and unconstitutional remedies—then they should be marginalized, along with their theories.

In these incendiary times, we should all remember our history. John Adams's Alien and Sedition Acts, FDR's internment of Japanese Americans, and Senator Joseph McCarthy's witch hunt from Hollywood to the halls of Congress are just a few of the moments that Americans now view with shame. An attack on our pluralistic democracy and constitutional government for short-term political gain is unworthy of any real patriot.

In many nations, elections are revolutionary moments. Heads roll, governments topple, and wars break out. In the United States, we celebrate our peaceful transitions. The Founders believed that free people could debate their differences, cast their ballots, and then work together for the good of the nation. The losing side may despise the victors, but if the rules have been followed, true patriots defend this outcome even as they disagree about policy or philosophy. An attack on the legitimacy of the winners is an attack on democracy itself.

In 2009, before he got into a nasty primary campaign for his Arizona Senate seat, John McCain said wisely, "Elections have consequences." This was the reason that Al Gore conceded the election in 2000 despite pleas for him to continue the recount fight. He thought it better for the nation to rally behind George Bush, a man whose philosophy he fiercely opposed, than to risk undercutting the government's legitimacy. This was the same reason that in April 2010, Republican Senator Tom Coburn of Oklahoma challenged a rowdy home crowd to stop demonizing the Democrats. To catcalls, he said his opponents were good people and challenged his own party to win on the issues, not through personal attacks on the opposition. To label a large portion of the nation and their representatives "un-American" as a campaign strategy is as unpatriotic as it gets.

In this country, we defend the right of citizens to hold opposing views and accept that our favored positions will not always win out. Our elected officials must be willing to share power and govern with people who see things very differently. This is not a matter of civility; it is a democratic mandate. Look at Iraq. People voted, officials took office, but then they refused to engage. To date, their government is a democracy in name only. Here at home, too many politicians proclaim "my way or the highway" and wear obstruction like a badge of honor; reaching across the aisle can earn them a primary opponent. I am not suggesting wholesale compromise for the sake of comity, but without meaningful debate and bipartisan cooperation, the system dies. True patriots should denounce such conduct, not applaud it.

Finally, both parties are willfully ignoring the greatest threat to our democratic process, further exacerbated by the 2010 U.S. Supreme Court decision in *Citizens United* v. *FEC*, a ruling that legitimizes the corporate takeover of American political campaigns. In private, our leaders know how corrupting big money is, but they refuse to reform our campaign finance laws for fear of losing influence and advantage. The same is true of our congressional redistricting laws. What should be nonpartisan is instead a battle between the parties to rig elections in their favor. All Americans must realize that these issues are critical to the health of our democracy. It is the people who lose out when special interests or tiny partisan groups control the outcome of our elections. To suggest that our elected officials should promote a healthy system is not naïve—our Republic was founded on ideals—but without a public uprising, these critical reforms will never occur.

All in all, this new Republic was a rather radical experiment. Despite their differences, our Founders were united in their role as guerilla fighters, insurgents in a revolution. When the dust settled, these men did not enshrine partisan beliefs or powers in our founding documents. Instead, the Framers gave us a strong but flexible system based on universal principles and ideals.

I have strong beliefs about the direction in which our nation should go, and I will make those arguments based not on modern political ideology but on our founding principles, constitutional government, and the lessons learned as the nation has evolved. Some positions will seem conservative and some rather progressive, but all, I believe, are consistent with the ideals at the core of our magnificent system.

Whether you agree with my proposals is not the most important thing. I welcome an honest debate; such is the essence of democracy. But as a patriot, I believe that our founding principles and system of governing are not negotiable. We must recognize the difference between honest debate over policies and philosophy and those measures that skew or upend our extraordinary system for partisan advantage. Such tactics may produce short-term gains, but in the end, everyone loses.

## II.

## *A Patriot in Search of a Party*

Ideology is the science of idiots.

—*President John Adams*

L ong before I studied our founding fathers or took constitutional law classes, I had my own vision of an ideal society. We're all products of our upbringing, and Texas left an indelible mark on me. I was raised in a Dallas suburb, but my expansive neighborhood was dotted with open fields and secluded forests, a trip downtown was a big deal, and by the time I was ten, most of my free time was spent on horseback at the local stables. Reluctantly, I donned dresses for school, but the tomboy emerged with the afternoon bell.

By 1967, my family had rented a farm to house our growing herd of horses. I hauled hay, cleaned stalls, and competed in horse shows across the Southwest while my classmates went to football games and dances. In 1970, we moved to our own property sixty miles north of Big D. Rather than transfer to the tiny Celina High School for my senior year, I commuted back to Richardson each day, but psychologically, I was at home in the country.

As a kid, I was also at home in the emerging Republican Party. In 1952, before I was born, Texas broke for Eisenhower. Unlike the rest of the state, Dallas County did not return to the fold. Conservative Democrats in Dallas continued to migrate, and except for the 1964 election of our favorite son, Lyndon Johnson, Dallas County was now a Republican bulwark.

In those years, I was too young to make a reasoned political choice, but I made certain assumptions about the GOP based on things my parents did and said and the character of my community. What follows are the perceptions of a child, idealistic and uninformed. Nevertheless, they shaped the principles that still guide me today.

Texas was a unique environment in the 1960s. Houston had the Johnson Space Center, but Dallas was the business and financial hub of the state. Texas Instruments was a technology giant. Universities were popping up everywhere. Republicans were visionaries— building, innovating, and investing, publicly and privately, in America's future.

You certainly couldn't pigeonhole Dallas residents. It was not uncommon to wave to a banker on his tractor Saturday morning and then meet him at the theater or opera that night. Dallas was a churchgoing community, but religion was a personal matter. No one quizzed you on attendance or the nature of your faith. Plenty of people found their sanctuary where Ronald Reagan did, celebrating Sunday on horseback or with a fishing pole on some quiet creek, and that was just fine.

I grew up believing that Republicans were the "progressive" visionaries who valued national investment in science, technology, and infrastructure. Throughout history, our federal government had directed the construction of major national infrastructure including canal and railway systems, the interstate highway system, and the electrification of rural America. The Federalists, and later, the Republicans were the leaders who pushed much of this through over objections from the Democrats. They knew such investment was good for long-term economic growth and defied objections from liberals who saw this as an inappropriate or unconstitutional use of taxpayer money. Our public dollars were well spent creating platforms on which private enterprise could prosper.

I understood that much had come my way through no effort on my part. I was born in America to a comfortably middle-class white family and was provided support and opportunities many others did not have. But taking these circumstances for granted was unacceptable. In the United States, achievement was not measured by someone's station at birth, or by bank accounts or social standing. Americans were judged on what they did, not who they were.

I was taught that all children, fortunate or not, would have a chance to succeed in this land of opportunity. The nation believed in a hand up, not a handout. Our good public school system would ensure that all kids had a solid foundation to compete in the workplace. Lawmakers were struggling to remove barriers experienced by women and minorities so that all people were judged on their merit. Success and respect were earned through integrity and hard work.

In the Crier household, this notion of American meritocracy was on regular display. My parents would tell my sisters and me, "You can do whatever you're big enough to do." We never imagined girls couldn't do everything the boys could. I learned to study hard and pursue the things I was passionate about. There were no guarantees, so the message was do your best, play fair, and roll with the punches.

My folks weren't big on rules. As in the Constitution, there was a framework for acceptable behavior but plenty of room to maneuver. That's not to say we kids were left to run wild. On the contrary, we learned quickly that freedom expanded with trust. If I stayed out of trouble and was home by dark, I was allowed to roam the neighborhood or disappear on horseback without accounting for every moment of my time. If my grades were good, I didn't have to abide by a rigid homework schedule. If I demonstrated sound judgment, personal responsibility, and integrity, boundaries were lax. If I violated that trust, then my parents would lay down the law.

My takeaway? Respect for social rules, often called "hidden laws," provides much of the order needed in a community. Concepts like shame ("Don't do anything you wouldn't want printed in the paper"), honesty ("Lying will get you nowhere" and "The truth always comes out"), and not cheating ("Nobody likes a cheater" and "You're only cheating yourself") were drilled into my psyche. The emotional consequences of bad behavior were as much of a deterrent as any tangible threat. And ultimately, the loss of parental trust could mean the loss of my freedom.

Individual liberty was cherished, but it came with basic ethical and moral responsibilities. If you couldn't be trusted, then more stringent rules would be imposed and enforced. If your actions affected no one but yourself, then have at it. Laws intent on creating conformity were antithetical to our basic freedoms. These house rules were a microcosm of the American philosophy. America was truly the land of opportunity and our political and legal systems would ensure fair access to the playing field. What you did after that was up to you.

Our Founders understood the value of religion in creating a moral, ethical society—in reinforcing those "hidden laws." Many of the early letters or remarks that are supposed to "prove" that America was founded as a Christian nation instead are comments on the valuable role religion plays in establishing and maintaining civil order. Even Thomas Jefferson, labeled a deist, agnostic, or atheist throughout history, believed that the teachings of Jesus provided the most exquisite moral code ever imagined. Yet it is indisputable that the Framers established no national religion. Instead, people were free to believe and practice any faith or no faith at all.

Despite spending four years in Austin, the state's liberal bastion, while attending the University of Texas, I never questioned my party affiliation. Yet as a student of politics and international affairs during the waning days of the Vietnam War, I had to confront some long-standing beliefs. "My country, right or wrong" took on new meaning as we debated the war and followed the Watergate scandal. I learned the importance of questioning elected officials when they abused their constitutional powers and watched Republican leaders like Howard Baker demonstrate patriotism over partisanship when they demanded that their president resign.

As a student of history and the law, I was determined to follow this path, rather than one defined by party ideology or popular passions. The person who emerged from this crucible was a card-carrying constitutionalist, an economic conservative with more liberal social attitudes who still exhibited Texas-style "don't tread on me" libertarianism.

I headed for the DA's office right out of law school and worked for legendary district attorney Henry Wade. He earned his fame as a tough lawman who prosecuted the likes of Jack Ruby, although beyond Texas borders, people might recognize him as the named defendant in *Roe v. Wade*.

The years I spent as an assistant DA were as formative as my time in college. At the age of twenty-three, I went from reading about government to actually wielding its power. The office was dominated by smart, cocky young prosecutors. We had enormous power and discretion to pursue justice in the name of the State. I used to say (mostly with affection) that I'd never seen so many people who could strut sitting down.

The Dallas DA's office was known for being seriously tough on crime, and many young prosecutors competed to rack up wins with long sentences attached, calling upon law enforcement and using the court system to accomplish these goals. It was a heady time, and

I learned that rules and laws were not enough. Without an honest commitment to our *system* of justice, people can misuse their power despite the best intentions. The ends do not justify the means, and how you play the game matters more than the score. These maxims apply to every aspect of our legal and political process. This experience taught me a great deal about the nature of bureaucracy and the need to limit government authority.

From Henry Wade, I learned that the people at the top of any institution set the tone and can raise or lower standards by example. A story that all new prosecutors heard on their first day was that of a talented assistant DA arrested for drunk driving. He called Mr. Wade from the police precinct. "Sir, I told them I worked for you. Could you . . ." Before he finished, the line went dead. His final check was mailed out the next day. Maintaining the integrity of his office was more important to Wade than the conviction rate of one prosecutor.

As one of Wade's felony chief prosecutors, I put many criminals behind bars for a very long time, yet my tough-as-nails boss would always support me if I had good reason for leniency or dismissal. Integrity, good judgment, and the pursuit of justice came first in his book.

Three years later, I left the office with my ideals intact but tempered by pragmatic skepticism about human nature. I firmly believed that our *system* of government was good; it was the *people* running it that need watching. All the checks and balances in the world mean nothing if they are not enforced. The more power a political party has, the easier it is to violate this system. A weak branch, be it the executive, legislative, or judicial sector, allows the same outcome.

For this reason, I get angry when politicians and protesters scream about bad government as if the institution is the problem. "Government is inept; it is inefficient, wasteful or evil." People seem to forget that *we are the government*. The problems we face today are of our own making.

Human beings are ingenious, compassionate, and generous. We are also greedy, callous, and at times, blinded by power or passion or downright ignorance. Our Constitution and Bill of Rights established a framework for government and provided strong checks and balances on power. With magnificent simplicity, these documents protected the people against tyranny by big government, an elite group, or a dictator while also guarding the rights of minorities against an impassioned majority. I remain in awe of this accomplishment.

Yet, as I argued in my first book, *The Case Against Lawyers*, lawyers, legislators, and bureaucrats can shape the rule of law into an instrument of tyranny. The ability to make, manipulate, and selectively enforce our laws can subvert the very principles we fought to establish. Many people today believe that regulations are the problem. Often times, the real problem is not the initial law or rule, but the way it is implemented. Necessary restraints are ignored or subverted. Loopholes are created to favor certain groups. Sometimes, laws actually encourage the very behavior they were meant to inhibit. This is an indictment of those charged with making and enforcing these rules, not the rules themselves.

In 1984, I campaigned for the 162nd District Court, a poster child for *moderate* Republicans. Despite a strong primary challenge from a social conservative, I was elected and then reelected in 1988. But things shifted dramatically during the Reagan years. President Reagan maintained his welcoming persona, but Republican attitudes and policies were increasingly harsh and authoritarian, exploiting cultural differences and financial inequities to serve powerful special interests. I joined the ranks of those who declare, "I didn't leave the party, the party left me."

Today, I am part of the growing number of Independents unable or unwilling to identify with either major party. Like many baby boomers, I'm moderately conservative on fiscal policy and moderate, even liberal on social issues. I believe in Adam Smith's model of capitalism, not corporatism—a distinction explained in the next chapter. I believe in true liberty for the individual while recognizing civilizing constraints imposed by the rule of law. I believe religion can provide a moral foundation for society, but our system of government is and should remain secular. I believe in strong national security but not militarism or imperialism. There are good taxes and bad taxes and good regulations and bad ones, and it is absurd to imagine that a nation of more than 300 million people can operate effectively without a strong federal government.

While this platform may seem a mix of ideologies, I believe it is more closely aligned with America's revolutionary ideals and constitutional framework than those of our modern Republican and Democrat parties. In the remaining chapters, I will track the evolution of their governing philosophies, demonstrating how quickly both parties moved away from founding principles and how different our modern parties are from their conservative and liberal ancestors. I have two major goals. First, I will challenge party faithfuls to examine whether their policies are supporting a truly conservative or liberal agenda. We need a healthy debate in this country, and both philosophies have much to contribute to the national dialogue. However, neither party honestly represents the intellectual traditions of their respective groups. Second, I will demonstrate to what degree both parties have abandoned American interests in favor of a single global agenda, one that is devastating our citizens, threatening our national security, and corrupting our constitutional government.

The major political parties that emerged in the early 1790s share some characteristics with their descendants, but there are key differences as well. The conservative Federalists were proponents of big government and big taxes; they expanded federal power to turn America rapidly into an economic powerhouse. They believed in a strong military, and on more than one occasion, used it on the American people. As the more aristocratic party, they believed that intellectual and economic elites should run things and were not particularly concerned about individual rights for the general population.

The liberal, even radical Thomas Jefferson supported small government, states' rights, low taxes, and individual freedom. He opposed a standing army and American entanglement overseas, vigorously defended civil liberties, and was adamant about the separation of church and state.

Since the 1960s, Republicans have sounded quite Jeffersonian in their seeming hostility to the federal government. Their themes are states' rights and limited government, free enterprise, family values, personal freedom, low taxes, a balanced budget, and a strong national defense. They argue that Democrats want a big central government, are antibusiness, oppose family values and personal liberty, believe in socialized redistribution of income through higher taxes, and are weak on national defense. Democrats defend a stronger central government, equality of all citizens, including workers and minorities, and progressive taxation. To them, Republicans are authoritarian, imperialist, oppose real personal and religious freedoms, and are aligned with America's corporate interests to the detriment of the average citizen and the environment. Both sides claim that their versions of liberty, equality, religious freedom, and family values are the true American interpretations. I've left out a few charges on both sides, but you get the idea. In several categories, it seems they've changed places entirely.

This is important, because we are frequently bombarded with rhetoric identifying one party or the other with our Founders and with the "real" constitutional America. Ideologues from both camps lump these illustrious men together as if the controversies, political debates, and major compromises they engaged in didn't occur. They ignore the vicious infighting between Jefferson and Madison on one side and Adams and Hamilton on the other, as well as their moments and methods of compromise.

Now, here come the Tea Partiers. They started out as financial crusaders, angry at Wall Street and the business elite, but that agenda changed rapidly when they garnered support from traditional Republican contributors like the billionaire Koch brothers and former House majority leader Dick Armey. Social conservatives joined the movement, bringing their issues into the mix. Now, this Republican wing is distinguished from traditional members primarily by a steadfast unwillingness to compromise. Tea Partiers were responsible for the defeat of Utah's longtime conservative senator Bob Bennett, whose reputation for bipartisan deal-making doomed his campaign. Other well-respected members like Senator Orrin Hatch are reportedly in their crosshairs for similar indiscretions.

One of the greatest senators who ever lived, conservative Henry Clay, famously said, "All legislation, all government, all society is founded upon the principle of mutual concession, politeness, comity, courtesy. Upon these everything is based. . . . Let him who elevates himself above humanity, above its weaknesses, its infirmities, its wants, its necessities, say, if he pleases, I will never compromise, but let no one who is not above the frailties of our common nature disdain compromises." For him, legislation was simply the art of compromise. He wouldn't last long in the current environment.

The sad truth is that neither party has real ideological consistency today or bears much resemblance to its political ancestors. Political parties and theories about conservatism and liberalism have evolved dramatically since 1789. One has only to peruse the last few decades to see major shifts in ideology. What was considered mainstream Republican politics in the 1970s is now labeled far left or socialist by modern conservatives. Nixon expanded the Great Society programs, established wage and price controls, and started the EPA. If he were running now, he couldn't get out of a GOP primary. Ronald Reagan raised taxes, increased the deficit and the size of government, appointed Sandra Day O'Connor to the Supreme Court, negotiated with the Evil Empire, and sought to eliminate nuclear weapons. Bill Clinton befriended Wall Street, ushered in major welfare reform, and left the nation with a large surplus. His strategy of triangulation—co-opting GOP policies to disarm the opposition—pushed his party to the right. The high-tech elite and many Wall Street bankers supported President Clinton's *new* Democratic Party, and their money and influence produced the desired results. Goldman Sachs protégé Robert Rubin led Clinton's economic team, most of whom shared résumés with the investment community. By the end of Clinton's second term, the line on economic issues between the parties had blurred considerably. In the Obama administration, these same Wall Street executives are serving as White House advisors and conservative Blue Dog Democrats are critical to any legislative success.

George W. Bush and a Republican-controlled Congress ate Clinton's surplus and left us swimming in debt. His team created the $2.1 trillion Medicare Part D, the largest new entitlement program since LBJ's Great Society, and spearheaded a $700 billion bailout for investment bankers just days before the '08 election. His administration increased the size of the federal government and its regulatory agencies. Virtually no net new jobs were created in the private sector during his terms. His war on terror compromised civil liberties in extraordinary ways.

While some call President Obama a socialist, others claim he's in bed with big business. If you look at his actions thus far, Obama is not so different from George W. Bush in several respects. Many of Bush's people are still managing the economy. Obama continued the stimulus policies instituted by his predecessor. While the decision to bail out the banks and automakers is worthy of serious debate, all of the actions implemented by Bush and Obama were advocated by "mainstream" economists—not Marxist rejects. Much of the TARP money has been repaid, banks and other leading corporations are reporting record profits, and General Motors issued a new public offering that returned much of the taxpayers' investment. Ninety-five percent of Americans received tax cuts in 2009, and in 2010, Obama supported an extension of Bush's tax cuts for the wealthy. Obamacare's mandatory insurance provisions were lifted from a 1990s edition of the Republican playbook, and our health care system is still dominated by private insurance companies. Obama kept Bush's military leaders in charge of our defense and instituted a surge in Afghanistan. He took out more terrorists in his first year than Bush did in his entire second term and is surpassing his predecessor in the deportation of illegal immigrants. He is progressing on reducing nuclear weapons—one of Reagan's most fervent wishes, and yet, daily he is proclaimed a socialist or worse.

The Democrats have joined Republicans for a threesome with Wall Street, and both parties promote the incestuous relationship between government and big business. Neither will admit how this union has corrupted politics on both sides of the aisle and has damaged the American entrepreneur, small business, our middle class, and the free enterprise system. Neither party cares about a balanced budget, as both cutting spending and raising revenues are needed to achieve this goal. Both groups increase the size of the federal government; they only differ as to favored programs and departments. While there is a theoretical difference regarding the use of our military, practically, the results are the same. As for religion and family values, both parties use the topics to inflame debate but avoid any serious action if at all possible. When it comes to the average American, well, we don't contribute enough money to either party to make a real difference.

The point here is that both national political parties have abandoned any consistent ideology. Their interests are more closely aligned with their pocketbooks. Just follow the money. Even the more independent souls are not immune to poll numbers and party threats. Both sides rely on our willingness to rally around meaningless catch phrases and talking points and pray we won't examine either their records or their real allegiances.

In 2008, Republicans suffered a major political defeat. Democrats crowed and claimed a mandate from the voters. Two years later, the parties traded places again. The GOP declared that liberalism had been rejected and promised a conservative agenda that would put the nation back on track. Both parties are misreading the general-election voters. Many citizens now recognize the gulf between words and actions on both sides of the aisle. What they are seeking is honest leadership that puts the welfare of American citizens and our system of government above all else. These dramatic swings will continue until one party gets the message and earns their trust, or, Heaven forbid, until this silent majority resigns from the game entirely, abdicating our democracy to powerful special interests.

Our crisis today is much bigger than the economic downturn, bigger than the issues of war and terrorism. This systemic threat to our democracy is an internal virus spreading without restraint; it is the greatest disaster we face. Neither party offers an antidote, as this would return much of their power to the American people—where it belongs.

George Washington knew this. He spent much of his Farewell Address warning people against political parties, calling them "potent engines by which cunning, ambitious and unprincipled men will be enabled to subvert the power of the people and usurp for themselves the reins of government." He described them as destructive of public liberty, saying that "the spirit of party . . . agitates the community with ill-founded jealousies and false alarms, kindles the animosity of one party against the other, foments occasionally riot and insurrection." He called on the patriot, the civic-minded American, to limit party influence in defense of the Republic itself.

Today, what the nation desperately needs is tough, independent-minded Americans demanding the truth. We need an honest assessment of our problems—really, we can take it. To admit that problems exist is not a denial of American exceptionalism; instead, it is a proclamation that our "can do" spirit is alive and well, that we can tackle and solve any issue. Saying no is not a policy. Stonewalling is not a solution. We need leaders who offer real ideas rather than meaningless attacks.

It is time for Americans to proclaim independence from stale rhetoric and divisive politics and join together to build our future. We need to quit asserting we want to take our nation back; instead, we must take it forward. We must examine the realities facing the United States and the world and decide how to tackle problems in the most American of ways—head on. We need to rediscover the sense of national will that has defined our greatest moments, leading not by force but by example. Realism is critical, pragmatism essential, but it is our ideals and values that inspire people across the world. We must practice what we preach.

With our founding principles as a starting point, and history as the truest guide, we can navigate the storms that rumble across our landscape. In the remaining pages, I will use this road map to examine our policies regarding the economy, national security, health care, and other issues now dividing the nation. Fortune will favor different agendas as power shifts from the Democrats to the Republicans and back again, but the overall direction we must take is quite clear. And as we move forward, we must remember that our allegiance belongs first to this extraordinary experiment in self-government, the United States of America.

Another statement by John Adams comes to mind. He said, "Remember, democracy never lasts long. It soon wastes, exhausts, and murders itself. There never was a democracy yet that did not commit suicide." I hope we prove him wrong.

# THE ECONOMY

As we struggle to emerge from a deep recession, it is time to examine long-standing assumptions about our economy. Politicians
treat us like Pavlov's dogs, ringing familiar bells to make us slob-
ber on command. Conservatives cry out "lower taxes and unleash
the markets" and denounce government intervention or entitlement
programs as a socialist takeover. Liberals argue that big business
has perverted our system and that regulations and protection for
workers only balance a rigged game.

As loyal Americans, we want to defend free market capitalism, but what exactly does that mean? When politicians argue for
or against government regulations, corporate tax hikes, or labor
unions, how do we process that information? Is our government
the enemy of innovation and prosperity or an integral partner?
How has globalization changed the rules of the game?

The true patriot must abandon knee-jerk ideology, and instead,
make an honest assessment of our economic history and current
predicaments. Did our Founders share an economic vision for the
nation? How did American capitalism evolve over time? Do current economic policies serve the interests of our citizens and promote the nation's well-being? Are these policies faithful to our
political ideals?

Armed with this knowledge, we can evaluate our future. Globalization and technological advancements have completely restruc-
tured the U.S. economy. Do traditional arguments on the left and

right reflect this new reality? Do their policies promote innovation, opportunity and job creation at home and America's true national interests abroad?

The economic health of a nation is a clear indication of its political stability and international security. Today, our Republic is at a crossroads; one path leads to a slow decline, the other, to a rocky and challenging assent. When choosing the road, ignore fearmongers and false prophets. Let history be our signpost and empirical evidence the guide. If in doubt, our founding principles are the nation's compass and will always point the way.

# III.

## *True American Capitalism*

You taught us that liberty is the same thing as capitalism, as if life, liberty and the pursuit of happiness cannot be crushed by greed. Your American dream is financial, not ethical. You have taught us well.

*—Chinese ambassador to President Bartlett's*
*chief of staff, NBC's* West Wing

No economic system was established in the U.S. Constitution, but American capitalism is practically a cornerstone of our Republic. Adam Smith's seminal text supporting free markets, *Wealth of Nations*, was published in 1776, the year America declared her independence. Smith's protest against British mercantilism dovetailed beautifully with Thomas Jefferson's political manifesto, and Smith's writings became the framework for our capitalist philosophy. But theory and practice are rarely in sync. Do we practice what he preached? We're not even close.

From the outset, Smith's revolutionary principles, like Jefferson's, were meant to maximize liberty and opportunity for a broad population. His theories were a threat to big commercial interests and an impediment to rapid economic growth. In a Faustian bargain, our leaders pay homage to his ideals, but from the outset, they have ignored his model in favor of national expansion and global power.

What we call capitalism is, in fact, the American version of British mercantilism. Ludwig von Mises, a libertarian economist, summed up its benefits rather nicely: "Capitalism gave the world what it needed, a higher standard of living for a growing population." Measured thus, the results have been breathtakingly successful, but if the goal is the long-term viability of our economic and political democracy, we are in serious trouble.

This was the very dilemma confronting the American colonies so long ago. More than taxation without representation, it was the corrupt British mercantile system that ignited revolution—just read the *entire* Declaration of Independence. Challenging such corruption was a major focus of Smith's economic treatise.

The Industrial Revolution had turned England upside down. Its old aristocracy was swept aside by powerful merchants. This new political elite wanted raw materials for their machines and markets for their products. Britain dispatched its military to open up trading opportunities around the world. England's government and commercial interests were partners in this endeavor, and Parliament insulated its businesses with tariffs and protectionist policies. The many British colonies, including America, were simply a good investment.

All of these colonies were expected to play by the rules. Britain had first dibs on their natural resources, even if better markets existed elsewhere. Rather than encourage local industry, England would ship raw materials home for manufacturing. The colonies had to buy back the finished goods rather than compete by making their own products. There was nothing free or fair about this trade; it was a one-way street.

Not surprisingly, private property rights, restraint on government interference, and the right to keep most fruits of our labor are all defining concepts in America's founding documents. The Framers didn't specify just how this would operate, but their goal was to create an open and fair economic playing field for all citizens.

Today, Smith's *Wealth of Nations* is an economic Bible, but in 1776, it was a blasphemous challenge to the big-government, big-business mercantilism of Europe. Smith imagined that fair and free competition would encourage a system in which anyone with talent, determination, and the will to work hard had a chance to succeed—the very elements of the American Dream. Briefly, his thesis goes something like this: The marketplace is self-correcting, supply and demand dictate prices, and consumers determine the winners and losers. It operates best without much government interference; people should be free to experiment and innovate. Like Lady Liberty, true free markets should be blind to wealth and power and thus free of corruption. Any little guy can take on Goliath and win.

But Smith included some caveats that are often ignored. His famous reference to an "invisible hand" guiding the marketplace is often quoted as proof that the government should leave the market alone; that it will self-correct without regulations and interference. But Smith was referring primarily to small businesses operating within the United States. In context, his theory is absolutely correct. Individuals and small, localized companies should be left alone as much as possible. When they look out for their own interests by making good products and responding to the demands of their home markets, they serve the entire nation. Because of their size, any dangerous or abusive conduct by them rarely affects the broader economy.

What the politicians and Wall Street guys don't tell you is that Smith was highly critical of "concentrated wealth and power." He was British and had seen what happened when huge companies controlled an economy, particularly when they were befriended by the government. Smith treated *big* business very differently in his writings, saying it was led by "an order of men . . . that generally have an interest to deceive and even to oppress the public, and have, upon many occasions, both deceived and oppressed it." He referred to powerful corporations as "unaccountable sovereigns" and said they were as dangerous to free markets as tyrannical governments. Citizens would pay for "all the extraordinary profits which the company may have made," while suffering from "all the extraordinary waste which the fraud and abuse, inseparable from the management of the affairs of so great a company, must necessarily have occasioned."

Smith supported necessary government regulations, labor and human rights, public education, and progressive taxation to ease the economic and social inequities he knew would occur. In no way did he advocate redistribution of wealth, but Smith wanted to ensure a vibrant system that benefited a broad population. Without these "liberal" measures, he knew that the monied elite would take economic control, and neither his system nor Jefferson's democracy could survive.

Thus Smith's faith in a free, self-correcting market was not nearly as broad as some would have you believe. He was confident his theories applied to a nation of small businesses, but not so much in the chaotic world of large corporations and international commerce. Big business was as adept at manipulating the free market as any government. Unrestrained, it had the power to shape society and governments for its own purposes. Finally, he stated clearly that a strong government, acting through democratic and legal institutions, was the only entity capable of challenging such corporate power.

For all these reasons, Jefferson was a proponent of Adam Smith's ideas. Jefferson was not interested in building an economic powerhouse to rival Europe. A gentleman farmer, he envisioned America as rather self-contained, isolated from the vicious battles for supremacy that dominated that continent. Individual businesses would not generate a lot of federal revenue, but since he hoped that local governments would do most of the work, this wasn't a problem. Major regulation should be unnecessary. Small commercial activities would not produce much harm, and strong community ties would ensure that most businessmen treated their neighbors fairly.

Alexander Hamilton thought this was all nonsense. He was thinking *big* and didn't have time for Smith's small-scale, go-slow approach. Britain's mercantile system was elitist and abusive, but Hamilton knew it was the engine that drove England's powerful economy. As secretary of the Treasury, he planned to use that very system to propel America onto the world stage.

Both his plan and its execution were brilliant. Hamilton set out to consolidate power in the new federal government by controlling the money supply, tariffs, and trade and by managing the nation's industrial development. Farmers and shopkeepers couldn't provide the revenue he needed, nor could they finance the commercial development and infrastructure necessary for America to play in the big leagues. Hamilton needed big money and powerful partners in the private sector.

Right off the bat, Hamilton proposed creating a federal deficit. He wrote, "A national debt, if it be not excessive, would be for us a national treasure." This public debt would centralize the taxing authority, tie the prosperity of the debt holders to that of the national government, and make public debt (the deficit) acceptable right from the start. With this money, he would build infrastructure, foster international credit, and spur capital markets. The funds could finance necessary wars and ease economic downturns. National security was so important that Hamilton asserted the right to direct, even nationalize, those industries related to the military.

Hamilton asserted he had federal authority to take over all of the states' Revolutionary War debts. Thomas Jefferson and James Madison strenuously objected. This dispute illuminated deep philosophical differences about governing, and Madison's support for a powerful federal authority waned. As he put it, "I deserted Colonel Hamilton, or rather Colonel H. deserted me; in a word, the divergence between us took place from his wishing to . . . administer the Government into what he thought it ought to be."[1]

Emboldened by his victory in acquiring the war debt, Hamilton sought to create a Central Bank to manage the nation's money. Again, Jefferson's crowd opposed him. They saw no constitutional authority for this institution and considered it to be another power grab by the Federalists. Hamilton argued that the Constitution embodied *implied* authority for his actions.

This theory was eventually tested before the U.S. Supreme Court, in 1819. The High Court was led by Hamilton's friend and ally, Chief Justice John Marshall. In *McCulloch v. Maryland*, the state of Maryland had attempted to tax the new federal bank, but the Court's decision made it clear who held the reins: "The power to tax involves the power to destroy. . . . [The American people] did not design to make their government dependent on the States." The Court affirmed Hamilton's notion of implied authority, ruling that the Central Bank was constitutionally permissible because Congress had the authority to "make all laws which shall be necessary and proper" to carry out other powers specifically granted.

It is ironic that the Federalists' first major judicial battle was won with this argument. Today, conservative scholars insist that a strict, literal reading of the Constitution is a historic tenet of their philosophy, but it was the "father of conservatism," Alexander Hamilton, who insisted that the U.S. Constitution *granted* rather than *limited* federal power and included *implied authority* for his actions. Thanks to him, this argument is now established law.

Throughout his political career, he sought to expand national authority and to govern with the aid of America's commercial aristocrats. In his early writings, Hamilton talked of natural rights and liberty, but he jettisoned those values when they threatened his powerful central government. Individuals and states were weak and unpredictable. Even the Constitution was flawed; in 1802, he called it a "frail and worthless fabric."

Biographers put different spins on Hamilton's governing philosophy. Ron Chernow called him "the prophet of the capitalist revolution in America," while others were more crass, referring to him as "the instigator of crony capitalism" or the "American Machiavelli." As for his achievements, the reviews are mixed as well. Hamilton's pragmatism and business acumen made us a great economic power in short order, something Jefferson's vision would accomplish very slowly, if at all. But in exchange, we abandoned our revolutionary goals: the creation of a political, social, and economic democracy.

Today, politicians preach Jefferson's tenets on the campaign trail, but on Capitol Hill, Hamilton still rules. The tight relationship between Washington and corporate America is stronger than ever, and Republicans defend adamantly the expansion of federal power when it benefits this union. Conservative pundit George Will recognized this when he said of his party's founder: "There is an elegant memorial in Washington to Jefferson, but none to Hamilton. However, if you seek Hamilton's monument, look around. You are living in it. We honor Jefferson, but live in Hamilton's country, a mighty industrial nation with a strong central government."[2]

Without question, Hamilton's conservative faction—first as Federalists, then Whigs—was the party of big business *and* big government, while Democrats remained faithful to Jefferson's platform of limited government and low taxes. In 1854, the Whigs became known as Republicans and, as expected, wasted no time reconsolidating power that had filtered down to the states under Andrew Jackson's Democrat administration.

Abraham Lincoln's economic advisor, Senator Henry Clay, was a worthy successor to Hamilton. With no apology, he famously said, "There has never been free trade" in America. Ideals be damned, there was work to be done. He ramped up federal expenditures on the nation's infrastructure, subsidized private corporations, and supported protectionist industrial policies.

During Reconstruction, the nation was stitched back together by powerful wealthy interests that capitalized on both tragedy and opportunity. Political and corporate corruption was rampant. Great fortunes were made as the little guy was bought up and cast aside, and federal money poured into favored private businesses to rebuild the old and create the new. Lincoln would not live to see this era play out, but he witnessed enough and became the first conservative president to express real concern over Hamilton's philosophy. In 1864, a quote attributed to Lincoln described a national threat even greater than civil war:

> I see in the near future a crisis approaching that unnerves me and causes me to tremble for the safety of my country. *As a result of the war, corporations have been enthroned and an era of corruption in high places will follow, and the money power of the country will endeavor to prolong its reign by working upon the prejudices of the people until all wealth is aggregated in a few hands and the Republic is destroyed.* I feel at this moment more anxiety for the safety of my country than ever before, even in the midst of war. God grant that my suspicions may prove groundless.[3]

Unfortunately, these concerns had merit. His world was still dominated by farmers and small merchants. Corporations were in their infancy, a far cry from our modern behemoths, but Lincoln could see where we were headed. For decades, the U.S. government had been partnering with commercial interests to build the nation, but Lincoln understood that the marriage was now consummated, and he feared for the Republic.

Today, our corporate and political leaders preach a conveniently edited version of Adam Smith to keep us from demanding restraints on the powerful special interests at the top of the ladder, interests that rely heavily on their close relationship with the government. Most of Smith's principles were abandoned before the twentieth century began, but by invoking his rhetoric, our officials can serve their real constituents with little objection from the peanut gallery.

This charade has permitted the concentration of wealth and power feared by Smith, Jefferson, and Lincoln, to the detriment of about 95 percent of the population. Today, American capitalism has morphed into a sort of dog-eat-dog economic Darwinism, and the big canines have rigged the game in their favor.

Corporations are now so integral to our economy that people forget how and why they were created, and how, through the courts and political favors, they redefined the notion of American capitalism. We cannot make sense of our modern predicaments without understanding their unique history and dramatic impact on our economic freedoms, national policies, and democratic values.

# IV.

## *The Rise of the Corporation*

The strongest argument for free enterprise is that it prevents anybody from having too much power; whether that person is a government official, a trade union official, or a business executive.

—*Milton Friedman,* Freedom to Choose *TV program, 1980, episode, "The Tyranny of Control"*

Our current system has little in common with Adam Smith's market economy, what we believe to be American capitalism. Reread Friedman's statement. Does that sound like the country you are living in? Right now, a handful of investment banks controls about 70 percent of the nation's GDP. We have corporations larger than entire nations. These paper tigers have been given various "human" rights but are protected by law from other obligations and accountability we expect from our citizens. In its 2010 *Citizens United* ruling, the Supreme Court decided that big businesses can directly fund "independent" political commercials during our elections. With no limits on their ability to campaign for or against candidates, multinational corporations can buy our elections *legally*. This is not capitalism or democracy. It is insanity.

I believe in economic liberty—free enterprise, free trade, and the ability to accumulate great wealth fairly, and then, the right to keep most of it. Like most Americans, I also believe that everyone should play by pretty much the same rules. Cheating isn't fair; getting special backroom deals isn't fair; making other people pay for your screw-ups while you cash in isn't fair; buying off the authorities to get a contract isn't fair. You get the idea.

What has happened over the last several decades is that the *really* big guys (*not* mom and pop businesses or even small corporations) have completely changed the rules. They use their concentrated wealth and power to buy off politicians, skate around regulations, abuse their privileges, and, sometimes, break the laws to win. When their politicians and corporate-sponsored "citizen" groups insist that small government and the market itself are sufficient checks, that further controls are a socialist plot to destroy democratic capitalism, they are counting on our collective naïveté to win the game. They are destroying free enterprise by abusing the very freedoms intrinsic to a market economy. Again, this is not capitalism; it is calculated corporatism.

Wonderfully, Americans are idealistic. We are proud of our leading companies, which have propelled this nation to great heights, and with it, the standard of living for many people around the world. So we often assume that because a corporation is American, it must be morally "good." But although entire books have been written about socially minded CEOs and the philanthropic efforts of certain companies, the fact remains that all big corporations have one stated goal, and that is to make money—period. They are not in business to do good, to compete fairly, or to benefit the United States and its citizens—unless those citizens happen to be shareholders.

If corporations were actually humans, here is how most would fare on a psychiatrist's couch. They are true sociopaths: smart, narcissistic, manipulative, and completely without conscience. Remember the wonderful parable about the scorpion and the frog? The frog agrees to carry the scorpion safely across a swollen river after the insect promises not to sting. The frog is stung midway, and as he drowns, the frog asks, "Why?" The scorpion replies, "It's my nature." I am not suggesting that corporations are immoral; I'm stating they are *amoral*—there's a big difference.

Ideally, the best interests of citizens are served by these institutions, but the bigger, more concentrated, and more powerful they become, the more individuals, small businesses, and even our Republic are irreversibly damaged. Much of that damage is concealed. It is only when an oil rig explodes in the Gulf of Mexico or fraudulent derivatives blow up on Wall Street that we begin to understand how much the taxpayer invests in these companies and what we *really* pay for their goods and services. If big businesses were subject to the same cost-benefit analysis that Republicans insist we should use to measure the value of social policies, most of them would fail the test.

For those of us who truly believe in a capitalist system that promotes economic liberty and free markets, it is critical that we understand the nature and evolution of the American corporation. The goal is not to disable or destroy these powerful engines of commerce, but to understand why they were created, how we have mangled the principles of capitalism into a corporate economy, and the enormous price we're paying for this mistake.

Corporations began as instruments *of the state*. It seems old-fashioned now, but in the 1800s, corporate charters were granted for a limited time and for activities that benefited the public, such as banking or building the nation's infrastructure—canals, railroads, and roadways. Incorporation was a *privilege*. It allowed individuals to raise money from investors and pursue expensive, sometimes risky ventures that they wouldn't or couldn't tackle on their own. In turn, corporate investors gambled only with the money they put into the company. If it went broke, they weren't on the hook for all its debts; they only lost what they had contributed.

Charters could restrict corporate capitalization, debts, property ownership, even profits. Large and small investors had equal voting rights, and shareholders could remove directors at will. Corporations could not own stock in other corporations. Today, half the products in a store might be manufactured by a single corporation, although each one bears a different company name. Not so in the beginning. You knew who you were dealing with and what they were supposed to do.

Instead of paltry fines, corporations that exceeded their authority or caused public harm had their charters revoked. Game over. Even if they did no wrong, the charter might not be renewed if they weren't doing a *good* job of accomplishing their stated purpose. The owners and managers were responsible for criminal acts committed on the job, and corporations could not make any political or charitable contributions or spend money to influence legislation.

Today, occasionally we read about citizens battling to keep a big corporation out of their town. That was not uncommon two hundred years ago. Communities were very much involved in oversight. Local governments and the citizenry monitored proposed charters and prevented or restricted business activities they opposed. Americans had witnessed the evils of British mercantilism and despite Hamilton's best efforts, local communities and state governments were determined to keep a tight rein on corporate activities. They didn't want wealthy owners to control markets and workers or influence elections and the courts.

In 1819, the Supreme Court made a ruling that challenged the states' authority over corporations. The states responded with new laws to reassert their control, but during the last third of the nineteenth century, corporations used an increasingly business-friendly judiciary to loosen their restraints.

In 1886, the Supreme Court made a revolutionary decision in

*Santa Clara County v. Southern Pacific Railroad* that has proved devastating to the original concept of capitalism. This is the case that bestowed "personhood" on these artificial business entities and gave them certain rights that until then had applied only to individuals. Horrifically, this colossal mistake has been expanded over the years, reaching a new peak in absurdity with the High Court's 2010 ruling in *Citizens United v. FEC*. This decision, giving corporations the right to fund independent political broadcasts in U.S. elections, will literally destroy our democracy if it is not overturned through legislation or a constitutional amendment. With enormous resources and an agenda driven by short-term profits and global rather than American economic interests, corporations are nations unto themselves, as you will see.

Given the move to expand corporate rights, the creation of "personhood" was likely inevitable, but clerical error may have accelerated this development. The *Santa Clara County* dispute was a routine local tax matter. In preparing the case for publication, the Supreme Court case reporter incorrectly summarized the justices' decision in the formal "head quote." He inserted something that was *never argued or decided* by the Supreme Court, namely that "the Fourteenth Amendment to the Constitution, which forbids a state to deny to any person within its jurisdiction the equal protection of the laws, applies to these corporations." It is worth noting that this court reporter was working simultaneously for the very railroad involved in this case.

Because of this error (and our tendency to read the summary, not the case), suddenly corporations were winning new privileges in legislatures and courts across the country. As Thom Hartmann describes in his book *Unequal Protection*, this "head quote" became black-letter law. Justice William O. Douglas would note with regret that "corporations were now armed with constitutional prerogatives."

Delaware and Maryland wanted more corporate tax revenue,

so to attract more business, they further eased state restrictions and oversight. They created a national race to the bottom as other states followed suit. Today, many states are teetering on the verge of bankruptcy but refuse to consider raising corporate tax rates for fear companies will move to a more accommodating location. Big corporations have played this card successfully for a long time, and today, they argue that the United States should engage in an international race to the bottom, giving up our higher standards involving corporate accountability, workers' rights, or the environment to entice big companies to stay in this country.

Some large companies, such as Standard Oil, ducked legal restraints for a while by refusing to incorporate. They operated as trusts instead. This legal designation allowed them to own stock in other companies, thereby creating enormous monopolies. J. P. Morgan, John D. Rockefeller, and other magnates assembled wealth and power with little impediment during this time—hence, the Sherman Anti-Trust Act. This act addressed only those monopolies that *illegally* restricted competition, not those monopolies achieved on merit.

Responding to critics of the act, Representative William Mason said: "Trusts have made products cheaper, have reduced prices; but if the price of oil, for instance, were reduced to one cent a barrel, it would not right the wrong done to people of this country by the trusts which have destroyed legitimate competition and driven honest men from legitimate business enterprise." Mason was defending true American capitalism against the Wal-Marts of his time. And sure enough, when the Standard Oil monopoly was broken, the smaller offspring (including Chevron and Exxon) were tremendously profitable and made Rockefeller the wealthiest man in America.

By 1935, one-tenth of 1 percent of the nation's corporations owned 52 percent of all corporate assets.[1] Many of these companies were already multinationals and operated around the world.

Before World War II, some of this country's leading isolationists were major CEOs who had very profitable operations in the Axis countries and didn't want to endanger their interests. Such companies as Standard Oil of New Jersey, Ford, ITT, Alcoa, GE, and Chase Bank played major roles in building and supporting the Nazi war machine. The power of corporations to influence American foreign policy was significantly expanding.

In its Economic Report to the President in January 1950, the Council of Economic Advisors calculated that the 250 largest manufacturing corporations that year had emerged from World War II with manufacturing facilities equal to *the entire productive capacity of the country before the war.* They acquired this size and influence through taxpayer help and government support. This is not Smith's capitalism at work; it is the corporatism that Jefferson, Lincoln, and both Roosevelts feared. Another Republican president would soon join their ranks.

President Dwight D. Eisenhower saw the national security implications of corporate influence on government and democracy. He echoed Lincoln's warnings in his farewell address to the nation on January 17, 1961:

This conjunction of an immense military establishment and a large arms industry is new in the American experience. The total influence—economic, political, even spiritual—is felt in every city, every Statehouse, every office of the Federal government. We recognize the imperative need for this development. Yet we must not fail to comprehend its grave implications. Our toil, resources and livelihood are all involved; so is the very structure of our society. In the councils of government, we must guard against the acquisition of unwarranted influence, whether sought or unsought, by the military-industrial complex. The potential for the disastrous rise of misplaced power exists and will persist.

We must never let the weight of this combination endanger

our liberties or democratic processes. We should take nothing for granted. Only an alert and knowledgeable citizenry can compel the proper meshing of the huge industrial and military machinery of defense with our peaceful methods and goals, so that security and liberty may prosper together.

In reviewing Eisenhower's original draft of this address, historians discovered that he first wrote of the "Military-Industrial-*Congressional* complex." Staffers convinced him that it was unwise to make such a reference, although this was a clear nod to the incestuous relationship that existed between business and government.

What began as an economic system designed to counter British mercantilism had become its twin. Powerful U.S. corporations now controlled a majority of the nation's commerce, ran Washington, D.C., and directed our domestic and international policies. They were given more rights in the late 1800s than many Americans possessed at the time, most notably women and minorities. By 1915, this comment in *Brannan* v. *Schartzer* said it all: "The legal rights of the ... defendant, Loan Company, although it be a corporation, soulless and speechless, rise as high in the scales of law and justice as those of the most obscure and poverty-stricken subject of the state" (25 Ohio Dec. 491 [1915]). When Eisenhower gave his farewell speech, these obscure Americans were still years away from comparable recognition under the law. I'm only talking about issues of equal protection; when it comes to competitive business privileges—tax breaks, subsidies, overt political power—individuals and small businesses can just fugitaboutit.

The myth that corporations are somehow equivalent to the human beings Adam Smith was liberating in his free market utopia represents possibly the most successful political coup in the history of the world. That so many conservatives, adamant in their defense of true capitalism, would fail to make this distinction gives credence to the power of the "big lie." They have so internalized this nonsense that, again and again, they are willing to defend transnational behemoths over the well-being of their own people and country. Today, our nation is facing a major economic crisis, yet Republican leaders are steadfastly insisting that we not only cut wages and services for most citizens, but lower corporate tax rates at the same time without requiring the reduction or elimination of corporate subsidies and tax breaks. Hell, we're actually paying companies like GE for the privilege of buying their stuff. In March 2011, it reported worldwide profits of $14.2 billion; $5.1 billion of the total came from U.S. operations. GE's tax bill? Zero, zip, nada. The corporation received a *credit* of $3.2 billion. Oh, by the way, since 2002, the company has eliminated a fifth of its U.S. workforce.

It was the GOP's patron saint, Ronald Reagan, who tried to close the tax loopholes on corporations in his 1986 Tax Reform Act. In his 1988 memoirs, he told Treasury Secretary Donald Regan, "I didn't realize things had gotten that far out of line." But by the late 1990s, corporations were back in control. Both parties have been complicit, trading tax favors for fat campaign contributions.

Just where do the American people fit into this picture? What role do we play in our so-called capitalist system? Let's take a look.

## V.

# *Valuing Human Capital*

Amerika has a consumer economy. Today, our nation's fiscal health depends more on increased consumption than on the production of goods and services. But average real wages for most workers have stagnated or fallen over the last thirty-five years, and good jobs are disappearing. Without employment or income, what's the key to our economic recovery? Plastic.

Since the early 1980s, each time the economy has dipped, we're told to go shopping. Rather than examine the decline in jobs and wages, our political and corporate leaders just craft new ways to extend credit to consumers. Perversely, consumer debt is now a valuable commodity to be packaged and sold. Today, we are experiencing a "jobless recovery"; corporate profits rise, but unemployment figures refuse to drop.

How did early capitalism morph into this? How and when did the rights and interests of our citizens become a threat to the U.S. economic system? What do current policies portend for American jobs and our political democracy?

In the late 1800s, aptly dubbed the Gilded Age, men like Vanderbilt, Rockefeller, Mellon, Carnegie, and J. P. Morgan were known as "robber barons." America's mercantile policies had produced the desired effect, consolidating power in a burgeoning industrial economy and controlling much of the nation's workforce. These big companies made a lot of money for the government, not to mention the graft paid to public officials, and they were rewarded in the legislatures and courts. However, American workers were on their own.

Exploitation and abuse were common. Employees in company towns became indentured servants when paychecks couldn't cover the cost of food and housing owed to their bosses. Private security forces like the Pinkertons were used to intimidate laborers. Just as Adam Smith had predicted one hundred years earlier, workers' protests made headlines while backroom lobbying and power plays by the owners were downplayed or ignored. A new breed of journalists, the muckrakers, targeted this vacuum. Focusing on the plight of American workers, these reporters demonstrated that the problems were not endemic to some shiftless, greedy underclass but sprang from corruption and abuse at the highest levels of business and politics. In 1906, Upton Sinclair exposed the dark side of American capitalism in his bestseller, *The Jungle*.

Americans have always believed that a strong capitalist class benefits working men and women; we accept great financial disparity as part of our system. People applaud when hard work, risk, and talent pay off; that's our shared dream. Over the years, citizens have tolerated tremendous influence peddling and special-interest politics in Washington, asking only for a modicum of stability and financial security in exchange for the promise of equal opportunity, not equal outcomes.

Our relatively passive population stirs only when political manipulation, corruption, and fraud become truly obvious; when social and economic abuses are clearly visible and the fallout is widespread. This was the situation as we entered the twentieth century. The budding labor movement won new recruits for good reason. The Socialist Party had its brief moment in the sun, peaking in 1912 when Eugene Debs won almost one million votes in the presidential election.

Instead of ignoring or suppressing these problems, progressive

Republicans Teddy Roosevelt and William Howard Taft decided to tackle them. To make any headway, this effort had to spring from the Republican fold, but these two presidents made many political and corporate enemies in the process. We owe them an enormous debt of gratitude. Rather than betraying capitalists, they knew when to check the excesses of big business and when to open the safety valve to release social and political tensions before things really got out of hand.

In Roosevelt's first inaugural address, he praised American capitalists at length, applauding their enormous contributions. He highlighted the many benefits to rich and poor alike and warned citizens not to target these titans with misplaced rage. Only then did he speak, rather gently, of the need to rein in certain corporate abuses and regulate or break up big monopolies. I've heard him roundly criticized by conservative pundits as a Republican turncoat. It is worth reading this speech to see how narrowly he drew his concerns and how much he supported the tenets of capitalism.

In his autobiography, he described this need to balance competing interests:

> I [had] been taught that [a man] should be honest in his dealings with others and charitable in the old-fashioned way to the unfortunate; but that it was no part of his business to join with others in trying to make things better for the many by curbing the abnormal and excessive development of individualism in a few . . . the insistence upon individual responsibility [is] a prime necessity. . . . But such teaching, if not corrected by other teaching, means acquiescence in a riot of lawless business individualism which would be quite as destructive to real civilization as the lawless military individualism of the Dark Ages.

Roosevelt reentered the political arena in 1912, feeling that Taft had betrayed his progressive platform and that corporate abuse was increasing. His rhetoric was much more heated as he led his Bull Moose third party into the race for the White House. He called for a ban on corporate money in politics. He warned that when big business calls for limited government and more power to the states, this is simply an attempt to fracture federal authority and prohibit any serious regulation of misconduct.

Roosevelt described another interesting dilemma.

> We . . . have to contend against two sets of enemies, who, though nominally opposed to one another, are really allies in preventing a proper solution of the problem. There are, first, the big corporation men . . . who genuinely believe in utterly unregulated business— that is, in the reign of plutocracy; and, second, the men who . . . denounce both the power of the [corporations] and the exercise of the Federal power which alone can really control [them].

This should sound familiar. When the economy collapsed in 2008, Wall Street was in the crosshairs, but then Tea Partiers and other fiscal conservatives were reminded of the long-standing Republican party line against big government. The one institution powerful enough to restrain corporations (assigned this task by Mr. Free Markets himself, Adam Smith) was effectively neutered, and the party's billionaire contributors, like the Koch brothers, sighed with relief. Smith would have wept.

Roosevelt lost to Woodrow Wilson. During Wilson's new administration, the dreaded Sixteenth Amendment was ratified; but the federal income tax was a product of Taft's Republican Congress, as was the Federal Reserve. The ability to control our national economy is an extraordinary power. Collecting revenues and manipulating interest rates and the money supply can produce a good investment environment or encourage speculative spending. Such action can also create or ease economic slumps. It is no wonder that our current Fed chairman and the big banking lobbies resist increased transparency. Money management is as much about politics as it is about economics.

In 1910, a powerful Republican senator, Nelson Aldrich, understood this and grabbed the chance to design a Federal Reserve. Some historians assert that he and a select group of wealthy New York bankers (the Money Trust) secretly structured the institution to give themselves operational control. Democrats held hearings about the meetings and ultimately demanded modifications to protect the public from these private interests. But soon the Federal Reserve got the chance to flex its muscles.

What happened in 1921 is exactly what occurred in 2001, with the same outcome. Faced with a recession, the government needed people to buy stuff to restart the economy, but most of the money was controlled by those at the very top of the ladder. The Republican administration opposed policies that put actual cash in workers' pockets, so instead, it pushed for cheap credit. The Fed responded by lowering interests rates and reserve requirements for banks. People would *feel* richer and do what was needed—buy more goods and services.

The government and the business community did even more to encourage consumerism. The installment plan was created, and between 1925 and 1929 outstanding installment credit more than doubled—to about $3 billion. Suddenly everyone could buy a car.

As secretary of commerce under Coolidge and later as president, Herbert Hoover brought business and labor into partnership with his Republican administration to promote economic development. He was the first president to push widespread home ownership, a tremendous boon to countless industries, and he helped develop a new long-term mortgage to expand the target audience. In the 2000s, this same tactic gave us the adjustable-rate and interest-only mortgages to entice less qualified buyers. Hoover supported Teddy

Roosevelt's Bull Moose Party and thought of himself as a progressive, but his ideas to balance growing inequities—like a tax cut for low-income Americans and a pension for elderly citizens—were rejected by his Republican Congress.

By 1929, the top 0.1 percent had a combined income equal to the bottom 42 percent. About 80 percent of Americans had no savings at all, but easy access to credit made everyone feel wealthy. If an economy expands indefinitely, you're okay; you can keep making those installment payments. But when it doesn't . . .

In October of that year, the stock market collapsed. On Black Thursday, $32 billion in paper values disappeared. The Great Crash came on the heels of a decade of deregulation, speculation, loose credit, and increased corporate influence. The cycles of boom and bust in America were now commonplace, but this was the mother of all panics. Over the next three years, national income plunged by more than half, from $87.4 billion to $41.7 billion. Unemployment hit 12 million in 1932—one-quarter of the entire workforce, and almost 28 million people had no regular income. Not surprisingly, there was widespread unrest and talk of revolution. This was the nation Franklin Delano Roosevelt was elected to lead.

Consistent with its policies since the days of Thomas Jefferson, the 1932 Democratic platform called for states' rights, a balanced budget, and a 25 percent cut in government expenditures. Roosevelt accused Hoover of "reckless and extravagant" spending, and of thinking "that we ought to center control of everything in Washington as rapidly as possible." FDR came in to office with, yes, fiscal conservatives to manage the budget and Treasury Department.

Historians still debate what caused the Great Depression, and just as many argue about the measures FDR took to address the crisis. Today, some conservatives accuse him of promoting either socialism or fascism. But hindsight is twenty-twenty. The emphasis, easy to criticize now, was on doing something, anything, to stop the bleeding and save the Republic.

As you read this, go back just three years to September 2008. Over a thirteen-day period, Fed chairman Ben Bernanke presented a *three-page* proposal for Congress describing Bush's emergency relief plan and asking for $700 billion. On September 8, Forbes .com quoted a Treasury spokeswoman about how the $700 billion figure was arrived at. She said, "It's not based on any particular data point. We just wanted to choose a really large number." Initially, the House rejected the legislation, and the Dow Jones plunged 777 points. Everyone scrambled; by October 3, despite cries of socialism, fascism, and government takeover, the plan was law. There were flaws and missteps, but perceiving imminent disaster, the Congress chose to act, to do something to stem the slide. Corrective measures would come later.

Similarly, when FDR took office, the first goal was, literally, to save the banks. Overall bank reserves stood at a mere $6 billion, with liabilities of $41 billion. Roosevelt proclaimed a national "bank holiday" until he could push a recovery bill through Congress. Roosevelt's team wrote out and then hand carried a single copy of the bill to the House where, after only a half an hour of debate, it passed and moved to the Senate. By 8:30 P.M., the president had signed it. Will Rogers said of those first days, "The whole country is with him, just so he does something. If he burned down the Capitol, we would cheer and say, 'Well, we at least got a fire started.'"

The Economy Act of 1933 *cut* government spending by $500 million. FDR's initial policies focused on jobs and wages—the "safety net" and social benefits came later. Democrats were not big on programs for the *nonworking* poor. Roosevelt's programs, the Works Progress Administration (WPA) and the Civilian Conservation Corps (CCC), for example, involved putting people to work for the relief they received.

Roosevelt's initial wave of legislation, the first New Deal, included the National Industrial Recovery Act, authored with help from major business leaders. The program was a big, heavy-handed, micromanaged mistake, yet initially, many large companies supported its industrial policies and permissible monopolies. By 1935, the program was gone.

Eleven of the sixteen cases challenging FDR's recovery plans that went to the Supreme Court resulted in programs' being declared unconstitutional. Maybe our system of checks and balances was working! These programs were an attempt to respond to an unprecedented crisis and restore the American economy. In hindsight, we can criticize, but *at the time*, there were Republicans, Democrats, conservatives, liberals, business and labor leaders all scrambling together to shore up the nation.

---

*It is common sense to take an idea and try it. If it fails, admit it frankly and try another. But above all, try something.*
—Franklin Roosevelt

---

The *real* Republican objection during FDR's early days was not big government, which Hamiltonian conservatives have supported since our founding, but its new focus—public works programs, federal assistance, Social Security, and concessions to labor that benefited the working and consumer classes. Throughout our history, when, for example, infrastructure funding was seen as assisting business expansion, capitalists were happy. When similar programs were seen as "make work" to create jobs and funnel money to individuals—that was socialism. Sadly, any current investment in our nation's infrastructure, whatever the justification, seems unacceptable.

Many of FDR's New Deal regulatory programs were of lasting benefit, although the *way* they've been used over the years has been both good and bad. We needed the new Securities and Exchange Commission—desperately. Consider these findings by a 1932 congressional investigation into the Crash of '29. By the summer of 1929, Goldman Sachs & Co. launched its third blind investment trust that held nothing of real value but gained 66 percent in its first month. By November, it was worthless. (Replace those investment trusts with some of Goldman's derivative products today—same game all over again.) J. P. Morgan testified that he used fictitious stock sales to "legally" avoid paying income taxes. Of the $50 billion in new stocks issued during the 1920s, fully half "proved to be worthless . . . fraudulent." Fraud, embezzlement, corruption, bankruptcy—the stories went on and on.

The Banking Reform Act of 1933, Glass-Steagall, imposed regulations to ensure banks were banks, not investment houses or gambling casinos. The American Bankers Association protested, saying that bill was "unsound, unscientific, unjust and dangerous," but our current crisis is due in no small part to the weakening of these provisions in the 1980s and the repeal of Glass-Steagall in 1999. Remember the original objections when you hear banks and their political cronies screaming about regulations today. It's just a broken record.

Of course, FDR's social programs are the source of the greatest praise and consternation. "Make work" programs sent electricity across rural America and left us with legacies like the Hoover Dam and LaGuardia Airport while restoring human dignity and giving citizens a hand up rather than a handout. Social Security was established to protect the poorest among us from poverty, a program whose importance increases every year as the value of human capital falls and our lifespans increase.

All of these efforts were simply acts that restored some balance to our skewed economic equation, a condition that Adam Smith guaranteed would occur with unrestrained corporatism.

Many historians, including Pulitzer Prize winner Arthur Schlesinger, Jr., credit FDR with preserving capitalism and democracy at a time when poverty, class tensions, and a failing economy made the American system particularly vulnerable. I can hear the howls from conservative readers, but he was simply following in Teddy Roosevelt's footsteps, just as George W. Bush's economists would do in 2008. Bush's Treasury secretary and Wall Street free-marketer Henry Paulson said, "to protect free-enterprise capitalism, I had become the treasury secretary who would forever be associated with government intervention and bank bail-outs." While promoting his memoirs in November 2010, George W. Bush echoed Paulson's admission. Each of these men understood that federal action was needed to counter the huge social and economic disruptions inevitably created by corporatism, action that would be less frequent or drastic if we simply heeded Adam Smith's warnings.

What is good for GM is not always good for the country, its people, or the capitalist system we allegedly defend; it's time we make the distinctions. By May 2010, corporate profits were hitting record highs and our gross domestic product (GDP) was growing again. Many pundits and politicians believed our economy was turning a corner. But thanks to globalization, this traditional sign of recovery is no longer valid. There is little correlation now between the GDP and the well-being of our domestic economy. *This is staggering.* For years, if American companies were reporting more profits and the GDP was growing, we knew things were getting better. We could anticipate reinvestment of those profits at home and the rehiring of American workers. But today, our GDP is inflated by revenue from our transnational banks and corporations. We claim these companies on the American balance sheet, but because so much of their profits is retained or invested overseas, the GDP no longer reflects the true economic health of our country and its people. Do you understand? When pundits and politicians and economists tell us that certain numbers are on the upswing and things are improving, either they don't have a clue, or they're simply lying to you. It's hard to tell the difference these days. But don't take my word for it. In the midst of the worst economic downturn since the Great Depression, U.S. corporations posted record profits. Enough said.

And sure enough, while big companies have prospered, small businesses—our major domestic employers—continue to struggle. Their problem is not an inability to get loans, too much government regulation, or high taxes. They can't rehire or expand until people start buying again, and the American people can't spend without decent incomes—unless they reboard the disastrous credit train. This, of course, is exactly what we're doing.

When will we get it through our thick heads that without a prosperous middle class, America's domestic economy cannot truly heal? For more than thirty years, despite stagnant or falling wages, this group has been doing its part—consuming—thanks to credit cards and two-income families. This has created a false sense of well-being for citizens and grand profits for corporations. It has allowed both Republicans and Democrats to cater to their big contributors in the name of so-called capitalism rather than face the truth about our flawed corporate economy: an economy based on low wages, more credit, boom and bust—then rinse and repeat. In these cycles, the top 1 percent and the multinational corporations do just fine, but most Americans and the nation itself suffer immensely.

Our government, particularly under Republican leadership, rarely hesitates to protect corporations, yet somehow, protection of our citizens is off-limits. It is not lazy workers or stupid consumers that threaten our economic and social well-being. As in the 1920s, it is the unrestrained growth of corporate capitalism that is upending the country. Balancing these interests does not mean confiscating and redistributing wealth or subsidizing people's lives, but these inequities must be addressed. You don't have to support the notion of social equity to advocate for the American worker; think selfishly instead. Without a broad middle class that earns decent wages and can legitimately afford to consume American goods and services, there is no sustainable market for domestic businesses. We can rebuild on credit, but we will crash again—soon.

There are legitimate concerns about labor policies, such as union pensions or employer-provided health care, but they should be addressed honestly and then corrected with a scalpel, not a chainsaw. We should discuss how this compensation has been used in lieu of wage increases, and how such concessions affect business. Companies can write off health care costs, although these expenditures are becoming unmanageable; we'll take up health care a bit later. As for pensions, they have provided all sorts of wiggle room for corporate and municipal accountants through underfunding and exaggerated investment projections. These future costs eventually should come due, although at present, corporations and state and local governments are trying to renege on their obligations. I'll also elaborate on this, but remember, many times corporations will make concessions or accept regulations that may cost them a bit, but they know it will cost small companies much more—a small price to pay to reduce the competition and buy time to legislate their way out of those obligations.

We need to have a truly intelligent debate on these matters, but we must stop the absurd demonizing of working Americans in the name of capitalism. Capitalism was designed to free individuals to compete in the economic marketplace. Human capital was an essential currency. It wasn't until the advent of the corporation that money, investment dollars, became the only form of capital we truly valued. Today, technological advancements increase productivity without the need for more labor. Globalization means that every American is competing in a pool of 6.9 billion workers. Add to this the current attack on labor policies, including the elimination of collective bargaining rights, and you can see that about 90 percent of American citizens are in a crapshoot for their future.

Things have gotten so Kafkaesque that in March 2011, Maine governor Paul LePage actually ordered the removal of a mural depicting American workers from the state's Department of Labor because *it was biased against business owners.* He also plans to rename eight conference rooms that currently honor historic labor figures. Democratic Maine state representative Diane Russell had this to say: "It is on the backs of hard working people that companies make their profits. . . . It is not enough for conservatives to undermine the rights of workers across this country; now they are literally erasing them from the halls of history."

There are solutions, and both sides will have to give on the issue, but the blanket condemnation of workers and unions is simply propaganda used to devalue human capital in, ah yes, a capitalist system.

We've allowed large corporations to redefine our entire economic system and pervert both conservative and liberal values. What most Americans don't realize is the degree to which corporatism controls the entire national landscape, subverting our democratic principles and affecting, even dictating policies from national security to health care, immigration, and education. Citizens need to understand just how far-reaching the implications are for everything we hold dear. When people are frightened and hurting, it is difficult to chart a brave new course. But the time is now, and the stakes could not be higher.

# VI.

## The Not-So-American Corporations

CONSTITUTIONAL CONVENTION UPDATED

*By permission of Mike Luckovich and Creators Syndicate, Inc.*

Americans have accepted corporate power and influence for decades as simply part of our economic system. Because we have mistakenly treated them as persons, as pseudo human capitalists, it is a constant battle to constrain the abuses to our political and economic framework. Yet, unlike a single businessperson or company owned by individuals directly accountable for their actions, these entities are shielded by laws and contracts. Major corporations are not integral members of a community, no matter what their marketing campaigns may portray. They do not live and work side by side with their employees and neighbors. They're not shamed by any pain they might cause to others; goodwill is just a quantifiable entry on the ledger. They do not experience normal social constraints on their conduct. Only rules and laws can provide those.

When their actions become truly outrageous, politicians do hold hearings and propose meaningful measures, but usually those plans fall away when the headlines disappear. National amnesia sets in, and last month's catastrophe becomes just an aberration or the fault of the government. It's so much easier to ignore reality and stay on a comfortable course than to question a premise we've accepted for so long, no matter how flawed.

True patriots will review Smith's writings and recognize his adamant distinctions between capitalism and corporatism. Much of his work seems almost naïve in our modern global economy. Just as we cannot go back to Jefferson's bucolic vision of pure democracy, there is no chance for the pure market economy Smith drafted in 1776. But his structure can be revised, and we can harness the power of great corporations to work for the nation and American people while still making great profits and serving the needs of investors. There is a win-win in this equation.

But everyone needs to get on the same page. For those who understand that Smith's theories specifically targeted the abuses of British mercantilism, the original corporatism, this chapter may be redundant. For others who actually believe big corporations and smaller players behave the same and should be treated alike, consider this: a free market is only as good as the integrity of its prices. If corporations keep pricing artificially low by ignoring or hiding their true business costs, then the market *cannot* work as it was intended. Let's examine the hidden costs of American corporatism and see what we actually pay for these laissez-faire policies. If reducing the national debt, the size of government, and the need for regulatory oversight is your goal, then you should get behind true capitalism.

Multinational corporations derive much of their profits elsewhere, often in places where few rules exist about their methods of operation. Even in the United States, much of the damage they do is unregulated or ignored by those charged with enforcing our laws. They can sell products cheaply because they do not pay the full cost of producing their wares. Any expense companies can foist onto the consumer indirectly is money they don't have to add to the price of their product or deduct from their bottom line, all the while advertising their "low, low prices."

Guess what? That we're not paying the real cost of these goods at the checkout counter doesn't mean we're not paying for them elsewhere. The American people give away national resources for pennies on the dollar, including oil, mining, and grazing rights, and forgo state and federal revenues through government tax breaks and subsidies. Our tax dollars pay for government research expertise given over to big companies at little or no charge. Public money builds private corporate infrastructure, and we shell out enormous sums to clean up waste and restore the environment while paying higher insurance premiums for the damage to our health. For thirty years, while productivity and profits have gone up, average wages have remained stagnant, necessitating an expanded social safety net to catch an increasing number of workers falling through the cracks. All the while, corporate CEOs line their pockets and call for even more deregulation and "privatization."

Just look at the price of gasoline. Economists calculate that the real price of a gallon of gas is about fifteen dollars. We do pay this amount, just not at the pump. This figure is reached when you factor in the direct and indirect costs borne *by the taxpayer* associated with the production and use of this fuel: federal, state, and local tax subsidies, protection subsidies (defense spending to safeguard global petroleum resources), federal R&D programs that directly benefit the oil industry, regulatory oversight, infrastructure expenses, and environmental, health, and social costs.[1] If we realized how much we actually pay for this commodity, how might that affect our personal behavior and our support for alternative energy sources?

A recent report by British consulting firm Trucost found that if the top three thousand multinational corporations had to include the *actual* cost of their activities—if they had to build into pricing the waste, pollution, clean-up, resource depletion, and other factors that lax regulation or acquiescence permits them to get away with—it would add more than $2 trillion to their cost of doing business.[2] Please remember, these costs aren't "created" by regulations or government intervention. They exist by virtue of the corporation's activities. The only question is—who should pay the bill?

It would revolutionize our system to demand *real* free enterprise and insist that these companies bear their actual business costs. We would pay more up front for their products, but in return, we would quit picking up their tab in all these other areas. Additionally, if these companies had to bear the costs, they might just change the way they do business. Reducing such damage becomes a bottom-line consideration. Without economic pressure, there is little reason for them to change the way they operate.

In the meantime, we also pay for countless regulatory agencies needed to stem the destruction. So many institutions demonized by big business were created in response to egregious, repeated misconduct that could not be stopped without powerful federal oversight. Remember, if any one state gets too tough, the company just moves to another without a single national policy.

Individuals and local councils might be able to handle Sam's Meat Market (a fictional reference!) when it gets caught disposing of rancid leftovers in an unsanitary fashion, but when a major corporation dumps chemicals into large waterways, ships flammable pajamas around the country, or injects foodstuffs full of antibiotics or hormones, some equally large group has to catch the problem, study it, figure out what the consequences might be, and then regulate and supervise continuing corporate behavior. This costs money, and taxpayers pay the bill.

Esteemed conservative economists like Friedrich Hayek and Ludwig von Mises acknowledge government's role in regulating the economy. Hayek says that "probably nothing has done so much harm . . . as the wooden insistence on certain rules of thumb, above all of the principle of laissez-faire capitalism." He recognizes many appropriate regulatory functions of government in our economy. Mises says that the failure to include hidden costs to our environment, health, and safety makes corporate pricing "manifestly defective and their results deceptive." Without making the companies pay for these costs, you *cannot* describe their activities as part of a free market system.

Another way we're perverting free enterprise is through continued subsidizing of these industries. Desperate for revenues, local and state governments woo big companies with extraordinary incentive packages. They waive taxes, build roads, even set up schools and housing for an influx of workers, only to have the corporations wring out all the benefits then move on. The communities are left with no new revenues, empty housing, vacant shops, and workers on the public dole. Depending on the industry, often a huge environmental mess is left behind as well.

Consider Wal-Mart, an excellent example of not-so-free enterprise at work. The American people have provided more then $1 billion in state and local subsidies to the world's largest corporation, including: "Free or reduced-price land . . . as much as $10 million for a single project; Infrastructure assistance . . . construction of access roads, water and sewer lines [at taxpayer expense]; Property tax breaks; State corporate income tax credits; and Sales tax rebates."[3] It receives these breaks while importing 60 to 70 percent of its goods from other countries. It is among China's top ten trading partners; the other nine are countries, not individual companies. Thanks to this lucrative relationship, thousands of American jobs have moved to China.

Once Wal-Mart arrives in a town, it dictates pricing from suppliers, depresses area wages, and forces out many small businesses, often by setting prices so low it loses money on certain items until the competition is driven out of business. The low salaries leave employees seeking food stamps. By keeping many workers only part-time, it avoids health care costs. Both full- and part-time employees often rely on the local emergency rooms for care—paid for by community taxes. All of these tactics are part of the reason shoppers get those low prices—but as I said before, we do end up paying, just not at the register. You can decide whether this is good or bad. Just understand that when someone argues for free enterprise, what passes for standard practice in the corporate world is *not* free market capitalism.

While privatization of state and local government functions has been underway for some time, budget shortfalls have increased this trend. There are successful private operations and joint projects where taxpayers benefit, but many times, the end result is higher prices, bad service, and worse. The corporate profit motive can create perverse incentives. On February 3, 2010, the *Wall Street Journal* reported on good news for certain commercial real estate. "Demand remains strong for one type of real estate: prisons. . . . The sector has experienced fairly high and steady occupancy rates for most of the recent decade [and] the outlook for the private corrections industry is positive, [due to] overcrowding [and] cash-strapped state and federal agencies."

Governments are between that rock and a very hard place. They can't afford to build the facilities, but they must put inmates someplace, so they turn to the only guys in town. Private operators are hiring prison security on the cheap. The result has been too few guards, insufficient training, a very high turnover rate, and voilà, more prison violence. Despite their savings, these private companies are jacking up the rates to increase stock prices and executive paychecks. Since the states haven't built new facilities and have nowhere else to go, they are stuck. That's the free market, right? Not likely.

Many corporatists might draw the line when it comes to privatizing the very stuff of life—our water—but not all of them. In 2000, *Fortune* magazine declared that water "will be to the 21st century what oil was to the 20th." In its 2001 annual report, the German multi-utility RWE-AG hailed water as "blue gold." Calling the United States "the world's most attractive water market," the company jumped in. The Republican-led Congress passed the Water Investment Act of 2002 and made federal funding for municipal water projects contingent on local governments' first exploring possible relationships with for-profit corporations, either as partners or by completely privatizing their water systems. But communities that took the bait began experiencing huge rate hikes and poor maintenance of their water lines. Citizens rebelled, and in 2006, RWE-AG decided to bow out of the U.S. water market. One company executive in California said, "People are just kind of weird with water."[4] Watch out. This retreat was only temporary, and corporations are salivating at the chance to control our water supplies.

That goes for our coastlines and oceans as well. Thanks to Sarah Palin, "drill baby, drill" is a familiar phrase, but it is not so simple. Any realist knows that the country will be dependent on oil for some time, but the April 2010 oil rig explosion in the Gulf of

Mexico and the more recent spill in the pristine Yellowstone River should give everyone pause. Big corporations want the freedom to operate as they choose; they know best until the markets collapse or millions of gallons of oil wash ashore. Then, they look to Washington and shrug. They'll take the risks and reap the profits, but when things go wrong, they're rarely willing to pick up the pieces without a fight. If these were small businesses, the impact would be minimal, but one critical misstep by gigantic corporations can affect millions of people and large regions of the country.

Those who believe the Founders wanted absolute economic freedom must understand that these men never contemplated tackling the likes of British Petroleum (BP) or Goldman Sachs, but Adam Smith did when he designed his market economy and insisted that only governments could truly counter such power.

Sure enough, when disaster strikes, you rarely hear anyone arguing that government should butt out. Instead, the airwaves are filled with complaints that Washington is too slow to respond, seems inept or ill-prepared, and should do more. Politicians who voted to defund critical agencies or supported the appointment of self-serving industry officials as leading regulators suddenly go quiet or reverse themselves entirely.

Some Republicans, like first-term Senator Rand Paul, actually called the BP disaster "an accident." He denounced big government, yet he wanted to absolve BP of liability and stick taxpayers with the tab. Let me get this right: Don't create, fund, or appropriately staff government agencies to prevent such "accidents," and don't raise taxes or increase the deficit to pay for clean-up when they occur. Just what would Senator Paul and his cohorts have us do?

You can't have it both ways. As big and wealthy as BP is, only the federal government had the manpower and resources to rush in, manage the clean-up, and mitigate the impact on people, the economy, human health, and the environment. Eventually BP may repay much of the cost, but this could take decades, particularly since it immediately pointed fingers at the companies that manufactured rig components, poured concrete, and operated the platform. When President Obama negotiated a $20 billion fund that BP would set aside for these costs, many on the right denounced this as socialism. Just what would you call it when taxpayers are told to suck it up, maybe sue, and then try to collect from the oligarchs?

Remember the *Exxon Valdez*? After twenty-two years, more than twenty thousand gallons of oil still foul Alaskan beaches, some marine species have never recovered, the herring fishing industry has collapsed, and communities that depended on Prince William Sound for their livelihood are still suffering. The spill occurred in 1989. The case went to court in 1994. Exxon fought the punitive damage award all the way to the Supreme Court, and then, after a ruling in 2008, it agreed to pay only 75 percent of the reduced damages to settle the dispute. Now, it is fighting over terms of that settlement. With their deep pockets, corporations usually can ensure that justice comes, if at all, in small doses long after the damage occurred. By the way, the single-hull *Valdez* was repaired immediately, given a name change, and began transporting Exxon's oil again within a year of the spill. When the Europeans acknowledged the danger of single hulls and refused these ships entry into port, the vessel was moved to Asian routes. This is how the game is played. Defending this as free enterprise, as American capitalism, is obscene.

Corporations must pay the real costs of their operations—what they use and abuse on the taxpayer's dime. If people understood the nature and cost of such behavior, they would never tolerate this warped version of capitalism. We must fund appropriate agencies and put in place serious regulations monitored by well-trained, *independent* officials. We must take serious steps against repeat offenders or those engaged in obviously negligent conduct. Measures would include prohibiting them from bidding on government contracts, imposing major fines, and even the revoking of corporate charters. Supporting free enterprise is more than loosening the reins; it includes tightening them when private power suppresses competition or acts in ways that are harmful to the nation.

Corporate political influence has thoroughly warped our health care system. The abuses can be countered without creating a government payer system, but without reforming the private sector, there will be no alternative. The big CEOs know this. Back in 1992, the Health Insurance Association of America (now known as America's Health Insurance Plans—AHIP) agreed to sell insurance to everyone regardless of medical conditions *if* the government required everyone to buy coverage and subsidized those who couldn't pay. Private industry was asking the government to establish an individual mandate, and the Republicans supported this measure. The association's president, Carl Schramm, said at the time that this was the "only way you preserve the private health insurance industry. It's plain-out enlightened self-interest." The insurers didn't have to follow through, as President Clinton's health care proposals were rejected, but Schramm's assessment is still on the money.

In August 2009, AHIP gave the U.S. Chamber of Commerce $86.2 million to oppose the health care overhaul law, particularly any plan that might include a public insurance option. Sure enough, when mandatory individual insurance was proposed in 2010 to derail any public option, the industry snatched this lifeline. Yet, at the moment they were rescued and were handed millions of new customers, the private insurers attacked Obamacare as socialism. The hypocrisy and deceit are quite astounding.

The so-called reforms in the 2009 legislation left a handful of big companies in control, and it shows. Our leading health insurance corporations remain exempt from antitrust laws. The reason for their immunity disappeared decades ago, but big contributions have preserved this abuse. People cannot buy policies across state lines, which further strengthens their monopolies.

Average U.S. health costs per family have more than doubled in just the last nine years, but there is more to come. In a 2010 report from Health and Human Services (HHS), the National Association of Insurance Commissioners predicted that the nation "will see rate increases of 20, 25, 30 percent . . . [already] some of the premium increases . . . are 5 to 10 times larger than the growth rate in national health care expenditures." The report revealed that "profits for the ten largest insurance companies increased 250% between 2000 and 2009, ten times faster than inflation." In 2009, the five largest health insurance companies "took in combined profits of $1.2 billion, up 56% over 2008," and the top insurance CEOs "more than doubled their compensation from the year before."[5] So much for a recession.

When Aetna reported that it was increasing payouts of claims from 77.9 to 79.4 percent of company revenues a few years ago, its stock price *dropped* 20 percent. Wall Street doesn't want them to pay claims; it wants them to make profits! In the spring of 2010, Aetna disappointed investors again by reporting profits that were two cents lower than the anticipated forty-two cents a share. Quickly, CEO Ronald A. Williams reassured investors by conference call that he'd jacked up prices and increased the profit margin. It's all about the stock price.[6]

And what about Big Pharma? Americans pay about twice as much for their drugs as citizens in other countries. We're told that the enormous cost of research and development paid by U.S. drug companies is the reason for our high prices. Let's check out their claim.

About 15 percent of corporate expenditures goes to R&D, about 40 percent goes into production, and the rest . . . marketing the drugs and, of course, profits. The reason those research costs are so low is that taxpayers, through the National Institutes of Health and university grants, fund more than 40 percent of this critical work. A 1995 study by MIT concluded that "eleven of the 14 most medically significant drugs developed in the US between 1970 and 1995 originated with government-funded research." That trend continues today.

And what do we get for our contribution? Here's an example. Decades before the major cancer drug Taxol hit the market, more than $500 million in public funds had gone into its development. Bristol-Myers-Squibb received all production rights, and the taxpayers—a 0.5 percent royalty. Despite our financial contribution, Medicare recipients pay about 2,000 percent over cost for this drug.

We are not permitted to import cheaper drugs from Canada and Europe, allegedly for safety reasons. Congress goes along with this charade to keep Big Pharma happy. But here's the truth. Despite the "propaganda" about possible contamination or knockoffs, these are the same drugs we buy at home, *the very same*. Can we get contaminated drugs from overseas companies? Of course, but actually, our "American" pharmaceutical companies do most of their drug testing and manufacturing overseas, with virtually no supervision by U.S. regulatory agencies. They deliver questionable and compromised results to the FDA, yet drug approval is rarely withheld. The premium prices we pay are very real; the notion that we get special protection is a lie.

Increasingly, drug companies pay universities directly for their work. This once independent research is now questionable, as it is funded entirely by the company seeking specific results. Until the 1990s, academic researchers in respected universities and teaching hospitals handled most testing for the drug companies. Now, this work is outsourced to private "contract-research organizations."

These corporations provide a turnkey operation. They "devise the rules for the clinical trials, conduct the trials themselves, prepare reports on the results, ghostwrite technical articles for medical journals, and create promotional campaigns."[7]

Most important, they almost always get the right results for their clients. If they bother to test in the United States, then don't like the results, they just double up on trials overseas, where patients, researchers, and results are more easily manipulated. "There's even a term for countries that have shown themselves to be especially amenable when drug companies need positive data fast: They're called 'rescue countries.'"[8]

In 2004, the FDA found that data for a new drug, Ketek, was falsified—one researcher went to prison—but only a month later, the agency approved the antibiotic, on the basis of testing done in Hungary, Morocco, Tunisia, and Turkey. In 2006, FDA safety official David Graham noted, "It's as if every principle governing the review and approval of new drugs was abandoned or suspended" for this product. Despite mounting evidence of (and deaths from) severe liver damage and other serious side effects, the drug remains on the market, albeit with a black-box warning about the dangers.

When a contaminated blood thinner, Heparin, killed as many as two hundred Americans in 2007–8, "It took months for the FDA, its Chinese counterpart, and [distributor] Baxter International to track the source of contamination to Changzhou." There, small family farmers were processing the pig intestinal membranes needed to make this drug—with virtually no supervision.[9]

"The annual American death toll from [FDA-approved] prescription drugs considered 'safe' can be put at around 200,000." This figure "dwarfs the number of people who die from street drugs such as cocaine and heroin [or] die every year in automobile accidents. So far, these deaths have triggered no medical crusades, no tough new regulations."[10]

If these multinational companies can research on our dime and test and manufacture overseas, and if the FDA is not going to enforce tougher standards for U.S. customers, then why can't we import these same drugs at half the price? Because politicians and regulators are allied with the big drug companies, not the American people.

Worse yet, Big Pharma repeatedly violates our laws and gets a wrist slap. In 2004, at the very moment Pfizer was negotiating a $430 million settlement for illegally pushing the drug Neurontin for unapproved uses and promising to never, ever do this again, it was busy pitching other drugs for off-label use. This is *criminal* behavior. Five years later, it would plead guilty again for marketing Bextra, a drug so dangerous that it was yanked from the market for all uses in 2005. The company received a letter denying it the right to market the drug for acute pain in 2001. It simply ignored the letter and marketed it anyway. This time the fine was larger: $1.9 billion for the criminal violations and $1 billion for the civil charges, a drop in the bucket compared to the profits the company made on sales.

"Marketing departments of many drug companies don't respect any boundaries of professionalism or the law," according to Jerry Avorn, a professor at Harvard Medical School.[11] It is just the cost of doing business. In the last six years, seven drug companies have paid about $7 billion in fines and penalties for such conduct. Then they go out and do it again. They make so much money off the drugs that even billion-dollar fines don't dent their revenues. Lilly was already a convicted felon when it promoted Zyprexa for off-label use. By the time it was caught, it had made more than twenty-five times the $1.42 billion in settlement penalties paid for the offense.

A felony conviction, particularly one for such blatant conduct, should mean revocation of the right to do business with government programs like Medicare; a second offense should lead to the forfeiting of patent rights. After that—three strikes and you're out—yank the charter. End of story. That WILL fix the problem. But it won't happen; our politicians are too indebted to these corporations.

As Eisenhower warned, the economic interests of major corporations also influence our national security and foreign policies. Sometimes they affect whether and how we fight—even who we fight. Our weapons manufacturers sell arms and defense technology to nations like Iraq that become our opponents on the battlefield. On more than one occasion, we've funded and armed insurgents who later use those weapons against us—just look at Afghanistan.

American transnational companies are working to improve their bottom line. If they need to skirt U.S. trade restrictions to trade with rogue nations, they just open up a foreign division or move offshore. Take Halliburton, for example. In 1995, President Clinton announced he was cutting off all trade and investment with Iran. Halliburton was making lots of money there. It had already been fined for violating export bans to that country. So what to do? Sign up Dick Cheney, the former secretary of defense, to run the company and then purportedly move all Iranian activity into a subsidiary, Halliburton Products and Services, Ltd., incorporated in the Cayman Islands. For this to be legal, the foreign subsidiary had to be truly independent of the parent company in Houston. Yet in 2005, nosy American reporters were told by company managers in Iran they'd need to talk to people in *Houston* about the issue. When this was reported, Halliburton responded that it was being "unfairly targeted because of politics" but then announced it was pulling out of Iran when its current work was completed. But it had just signed a long-term gas deal that would take years to complete, a contract that was issued as U.S. troops were dying from explosives believed to originate in Iran.

Trade sanctions are rarely enforced, as America's commercial interests often trump national security. Our government officials continue to award contracts to U.S. companies that make billions of dollars supporting Iran's oil, energy, and technology industries. William A. Reinsch, president of the National Foreign Trade Council, had the temerity to assert that if American companies were to lose the work in these countries, it would simply go to foreign companies—the old "might as well be us making the money" argument.[12]

Yes, it's all about the money. The companies that dominate the Iraq and Afghanistan war effort are, to be polite, rather tight with individuals who managed the Bush administration, but the Democrats are more than complicit. Their big-givers list looks much like that of the GOP. Corporate donations follow power more than political philosophy.

Our global military presence requires both a powerful federal government and a mammoth defense industry. When big defense companies become indispensable, we should not be surprised at their political clout. But today, the boundaries are increasingly blurred and it's hard to tell just who is working for whom. The revolving door between government offices, the lobbying sector, and corporate jobs is spinning out of control.

With his hiring of top CEOs as his financial advisors, President Obama is giving George W. Bush a run for his money, but Dick Cheney remains the most high-profile example of the incestuous relationship between government and corporate America, going from defense secretary to Halliburton CEO and back to Blair House as vice president of the United States. But there is more to this story.

When Cheney joined Halliburton, many retired generals and top staffers joined him. They stayed on when he returned to Washington, becoming the go-to guys managing contract solicitation and walking the halls of Congress to ensure that Halliburton remained a leading player in our military operations.

Additionally, these generals and other retired military leaders were paid by the Pentagon, military contractors, and lobbyists to "sell" the Iraq and Afghanistan wars to the American people. Appearing regularly on TV, they were identified only as decorated war heroes, not as company flacks. While reports had surfaced in the past, it was David Barstow's 2008 Pulitzer Prize–winning series for the *New York Times* entitled *Message Machine* that exposed the magnitude of the influence-peddling and government propaganda that was passed off as unbiased expertise. This scandal is just the tip of the iceberg; the practice occurs in every industry and on every news network. Sadly, the more respected the individual, the more valuable he or she is as a pitch person. If you are being paid to promote a certain position, it doesn't make your argument wrong, but as we say in court, "It goes to the credibility of the witness." Viewers should have this information before considering their message, and credible media outlets are duty bound to provide it.

As with defense contractors, other industries love to manage the very agencies designed to supervise and regulate their activities. Despite the obvious conflicts, this practice has been commonplace for many years. In the Bush administration, former heads of mining, petroleum, and pharmaceutical companies were running our Department of Interior, the EPA, and the FDA. We know how that worked out, most memorably with the BP oil rig explosion.

Corporate incest in the Mineral Management Services (MMS), the agency charged with regulating offshore drilling, was a major cause of the BP incident in 2010. In September 2008, the Interior Department catalogued unethical and criminal conduct by MMS regulators, and the *New York Times* summarized its findings: "a dysfunctional organization that has been riddled with conflicts of interest, unprofessional behavior and a free-for-all atmosphere for much of the Bush administration's watch."[13] Clinton had appointed an industry insider to run the division, and Bush did the same. No changes were made by Obama until the offshore drilling rig exploded.

Today, EPA officials are considering whether to bar BP from receiving government contracts. Ah, finally. As in the 1800s, we do have a method of countering all the corporate fraud and abuse—stop doing business with offending companies. We should be challenging such overt conflict of interest on both sides of the aisle. Our top officials must represent the best interests of the country and her people. The revolving door should be locked for several years when an elected official or top staffer leaves government service. But even that is not enough.

In her extraordinary book *Shadow Elite: How the World's New Power Brokers Undermine Democracy, Government and the Free Market,* Janine Wedel documents the almost complete melding of big capitalism, our government, and other leading public institutions. Wedel describes a new breed of free agents, an enormous contingent of private contractors who now make up *three-fourths* of the people doing the work of our federal government. Some work for corporations, some for consulting firms, think tanks, or non-profits, and some work just for themselves, freelancing their knowledge and influence to the highest bidder.

These people aren't just doing the bidding of the government; they're way outside that box. They are writing laws, drafting budgets, and creating policies that protect their personal and corporate interests. They are running security databases, performing intelligence functions, and supervising bailout and stimulus programs. Labeled consultants or advisors, they hold enormous power but have almost no accountability.

Goldman Sachs, nicknamed "Government Sachs," is the poster child for these relationships. Founded in 1869, it has produced heads of the NYSE and World Bank and countless presidential advisors. More recently, both Clinton and Bush appointed Goldman employees as secretary of the Treasury—Robert Rubin, followed by Henry Paulson. When our economy blew up in 2008, Bush and then Obama sought recovery advice from GS executives, the very people instrumental in creating this disaster. Paulson's old buddies were the go-to guys in devising the emergency actions he took in the fall of 2008. When sweetheart deals with companies like AIG became public, Goldman's fingerprints were all over the favors.

Despite the obvious influence, the corruption, and the buying of government policy, the U.S. Supreme Court decision in *Citizens United* v. *FEC* chose simply to legalize such activity. Some pundits applauded this decision as upholding the First Amendment; I cannot agree. The money, access, and influence have now been magnified exponentially by the ability to bombard voters with messages delivered through the (corporate) media. While foreign companies still can't run political ads, their American subsidiaries sure can. When big companies pour money into our campaigns, you'd better ask yourself, just who are they working for?

Despite this obvious corruption of our election system, I used to believe that the American people would win out. After all, you and I have the same vote as a billionaire CEO. I didn't want my choices restricted by term limits. I've changed my mind. Our elections and political process are so corrupted by money that we've reached a point where complete public funding of campaigns and term limits are the *only* way to regain our democracy.

---

*The first truth is that the liberty of a democracy is not safe if the people tolerate the growth of private power to a point where it becomes stronger than their democratic state itself. That, in its essence, is fascism.*
—Franklin D. Roosevelt, addressing Congress, April 29, 1938

---

# VII.

## *The Great Recession*

The money powers prey upon the nation in times of peace and conspire against it in times of adversity. It is more despotic than a monarchy, more insolent than autocracy, and more self-ish than bureaucracy. It denounces as public enemies, all who question its methods or throw light upon its crimes.

—*Abraham Lincoln*

North Korea executed its finance and planning department chief last week as punishment for the country's failed currency reform.

—*AP, Seoul, March 18, 2010*

Since 1980, the U.S. economic system has shifted under our feet. Americans have been content to consume their way into a narcoleptic stupor while transnational corporations led by the financial industry have taken over the planet. As we've seen, their interests conflict directly with those of democracy, genuine free enterprise, and often, the well-being of our nation and its citizens. Those of us who believe in traditional values, economic liberty, and the role of individuals in the Republic have our work cut out for us, but we have the power to change the road we're on.

First, we must quit salivating like Pavlov's dogs when we hear phrases like "limited government, low taxes, and free trade." We must stop voting on the rhetoric without examining the record. Remember Reagan's "Trust, but verify."

Forget what you've been conditioned to believe is the liberal or conservative approach—both sides push a modern narrative that ignores real democratic values. Instead, take a cold hard look at the facts and then ask: What do the Constitution and the rule of law require? Do political parties advocate policies that would achieve their stated goals, and do those policies encourage or violate our fundamental principles? How do those programs work in the real world and do the results truly benefit the nation as a whole? Applying this test to the recent economic meltdown produces rather interesting results.

What follows is a bit of a slog. After all, economics is affectionately known as the "dismal science." But without a basic understanding of recent events, we cannot evaluate what politicians and pundits are saying or make rational decisions about where we should go in the future. So stay with me—you'll discover just how titillating and terrifying the financial world can be.

The political ideology resurrected by Ronald Reagan and Margaret Thatcher in the 1980s was that of pure laissez-faire economics—what Reagan called "the magic of the marketplace." These conservative leaders believed fervently that markets were self-correcting and that everyone is best served if participants can act in their own self-interest unimpeded by regulations. Today this notion is often referred to as market fundamentalism.

It is called "fundamentalism" for a reason. It takes the very complex world of global economics and reduces it to a few noble sound bites—free markets, fair trade. Things are portrayed as good (private enterprise) and bad (big government). Actual results and long-term repercussions are usually ignored. Nobel Prize–winning economist Joseph E. Stiglitz has declared our current crisis as the moment when we can finally abandon this model: "The fall of Wall Street is to market fundamentalism what the fall of the Berlin Wall was to communism."[1]

A quick review: First, as Adam Smith made clear, laissez-faire policies work rather well on a small scale—for individuals and small businesses in a *domestic* economy—but not in the global world of multinational corporations. Second, we have *never* had a free market economy. Hamilton won the fight to pattern our economy on British mercantilism. He believed the wealthy elite knew what was best for the masses. Average citizens could cherish personal freedoms and lead comfortable lives while the real brains, the upper echelon, would manage the serious business of the country. They would make the big decisions and big bucks and the rest of us were meant to tend our farms and shops and families—and behave.

This has been our system, with minor deviations, for more than two hundred years. Sometimes economic or social injustice escalates to the point that the "people" must be tended to (for example, with Social Security or civil rights legislation), but when we're pacified, the top dogs can get back to work. It is amazing that average citizens still have any influence at all; for that, you can thank Jefferson and Madison and our collective belief in the Declaration of Independence, the Constitution, and the Bill of Rights.

I've been calling for a peaceful revolution for years. I was thrilled when the Tea Partiers started to march, objecting to Wall Street's bailout as Main Street crumbled. But soon, they lost the plot. Accepting the flawed absolutist's view that big government is bad and American business is good, they refused to look past the ideology and see the facts. Even worse, they lumped a social agenda—guns, gays, and God—into the conversation, and suddenly, we're right back to the tried and true equation: traditional values equals free enterprise equals deregulation equals Republican policies. This rather brilliant political tactic has convinced large numbers to vote against their own economic interests for decades. I'm not saying present-day Democrats are the economic alternative, but the Tea Party candidates have yet to create a rational, thoughtful platform. When they veered from the economic warpath, they staggered back into the GOP cultural fold, further radicalizing the party's positions in the process.

But if Republicans led us into this nightmare, Democrats are more than mere accessories to the crimes; their fingerprints are all over the place. Bill Clinton welcomed Wall Street into his administration and congressional Democrats reaped the rewards in their campaign coffers. They tasted serious corporate power and they liked it. A fellow by the name of Henry Grumwald once said, "Sometimes the followers must lead until the leaders follow." Now is the time to abandon party rhetoric and see the truth.

If we look at economics through a historical lens and not an ideological one, hundreds of years of financial boom and bust cycles establish a very consistent pattern. Does this sound familiar?

> Each separate panic has had its own distinctive features, but all have resembled each other in occurring immediately after a period of apparent prosperity, the hollowness of which it has exposed. So uniform is this sequence, that whenever we find ourselves under circumstances that enable the acquisition of rapid fortunes, otherwise than by the road of plodding industry, we may almost be justified in auguring that the time for panic is at hand.

That was written in 1859 and described a British crash that was created by "a new breed of growth-hungry executives, anxious to expand their loan books rapidly [through short-term borrowing for] mortgages at the top of a house-price bubble."[2]

Richard Lambert of the *Financial Times* examined eighteen

banking crises in industrial countries since World War II and found stunning parallels to our current situation. "Financial shocks in the past have often been preceded by periods of financial deregulation. . . . Low inflation leads to low interest rates and the accumulation of real assets [such as houses]. That in turn leads investors to take bigger risks in order to secure a higher return on their investments." Lambert also noted the moral hazard that is created when we rescue the investors—"Bailing bankers out of trouble will only encourage them to be even more irresponsible in the future."

America suffers from national amnesia. These economic crises happen regularly, and each time things start looking better, we reboard the roller coaster without checking the brakes. We like to go fast!

Despite two centuries of empirical evidence to the contrary, Ronald Reagan believed that deregulating the financial industry would solve the economic troubles we were experiencing in the late 1970s. The savings and loan sector was eager to expand, to move beyond the boring world of home loans and compete directly with big bankers across the financial spectrum. S&L executives wanted the chance to speculate in real estate and make some *real* money, and they wanted to do so with no strings attached. Their wish list included lax regulation, limited reporting requirements, lowered capitalization ratios, and, of course, government guarantees if things went bad. They got all of that and much more.

When the Garn–St. Germain Depository Institutions Act passed in 1982, President Reagan said, "[This bill is] the most important legislation for financial institutions in fifty years. All in all, I think we've hit the jackpot." Some jackpot—in less than seven years, the industry was gutted. Using their new freedom, many S&Ls engaged in wild speculation and major fraud. Corrupt entrepreneurs jumped in to make a fast buck. Average Joes learned how to flip properties. The bailout price tag exceeded $180 billion. Sounds like chump change now.

What lesson did our politicians learn from this crisis? More deregulation! In 1987, Federal Reserve chairman Paul Volcker was the voice of reason (just as he is today). He objected to easing the Glass-Steagall rules that had kept our banking and securities businesses separate since 1933. Remember, these rules came about because the last time these industries moved in together, we experienced the Crash of '29 and the Great Depression. The vice chairman of Citicorp, Thomas Theobald, argued that the SEC and ratings agencies would keep the expanding financial mergers in check. Hah! The SEC had been defanged by the Republicans, and the ratings agencies were paid by the very companies they monitored. Theobald was not worried. Volcker was outvoted.

That same year, Alan Greenspan succeeded Volcker. He was completely in sync with Reagan's market fundamentalism. One of Greenspan's long-time mentors was Ayn Rand, the self-proclaimed radical and author of *Atlas Shrugged*. She was the ultimate purist, advocating uncontrolled, unregulated capitalism, though she rightly called this "egoism." A child of communist Russia, she poured her fear and disgust for government into her work. She perverted Adam Smith's "invisible hand" into her "virtue of selfishness" and defended an ugly dog-eat-dog world: The masses were servile and insignificant, government was invasive and usually malevolent. Unrestrained, amoral captains of industry were the true American heroes. Her theories swayed me in my teens, a time when renegade individualism stirs the blood, but time and experience convinced me that she was wildly misguided and that Thomas Jefferson, James Madison, and Adam Smith were right.

Although her philosophy has never been fully implemented, we've suffered its repercussions at the hands of powerful apprentices like Greenspan. This was brought home to the world when on October 26, 2008, Greenspan publicly and sheepishly acknowledged his misplaced idolatry for Rand. Testifying before Congress, he apologized for his failure to monitor and regulate the U.S. financial industry. He professed shock that Wall Street execs might burn the house down just to make a buck, but this mea culpa came too late.

Back in 1987, Greenspan wasted no time expanding the loophole to allow banks to engage in securities activities. By the nineties, the huge "financial services industry" was fully integrated—investment bankers, credit card companies, and mortgage lenders were all in bed together with minimal supervision.

Not only did Congress deregulate this industry, but they ensured that the regulatory agencies were defunded and understaffed. This is a great little trick. If you want to seem diligent, keep the regulatory agencies for appearances but hog-tie them so they can't do their jobs. During the most recent Bush administration, SEC employees were going to Kinko's because they didn't have copy machines . . . and these guys were supposed to take on Bernie Madoff and Goldman Sachs?

Another useful scam is to have ratings agencies like Moody's and Standard and Poor's earn their paychecks from the very companies they are evaluating. That makes a lot of sense, doesn't it? How seriously will you investigate the guys who pay your salaries or promise a more lucrative job sometime in the future?

Senator Phil Gramm, Enron's man on the hill, led the move to further liberate the financial industry with the Gramm-Leach-Bliley Act (GLBA)—the Financial Services Modernization Act of 1999. Critics warned that by linking the banking and insurance systems to the volatility of Wall Street, Congress was inviting catastrophe. The *Wall Street Journal* didn't see it that way and applauded this development with the headline, "Finally, 1929 Begins to Fade."

Kenneth Guenther, executive vice president of Independent Community Bankers of America, knew what this meant for traditional lending practices. He stated it bluntly. "We're moving to an oligopolistic situation," and a handful of powerful Wall Street institutions would soon control the market.

Community bankers knew their customers—who was creditworthy and who wasn't. Because they had to keep their loans on the books rather than bundling them and selling them off, sloppy lending or fraudulent practices would bring down the bank. They lived and worked alongside depositors, so integrity was critical. If they hurt their neighbors, they paid a price. They made a good living, produced healthy returns for investors, and contributed enormously to their communities. Increasing revenue was not their sole motivation.

To Wall Street honchos, these little guys were chumps. The big boys would drive the nation's economic engine and boost the GDP. Revenues and share prices would rise. They would swamp the global competition. And they would get very, very rich.

This was the conversation in the back room, but the public heard something quite different. Supporters of Gramm's legislation emphasized the magic words "free markets." Deregulation would spark competition, improve customer service, and reduce costs. America's financial industry could fairly compete only if regulatory shackles were removed. More capital would be available for small businesses, and profits would do more than trickle down, they would enrich us all. By now, you know the pitch.

It didn't matter that history had proved otherwise, time and again. Without some restraints in place, deregulation encourages industry consolidation. Then, prices go up. This was all about power and money for those at the top; it had *nothing* to do with improving service for the average American or financing the growth of U.S. business.

Despite laws on the books prohibiting megamergers, regulators ignored them for years. In 1998, Citicorp announced a multibillion-dollar merger with Travelers Group to form Citigroup. Laws required the new company to divest many important assets, but its executives ignored the rules. By now, leading Democrats were on board; the money from big business was too darn attractive. Citibank knew the fix was in.

After resigning as Clinton's Treasury secretary, Robert Rubin helped broker the final deal to pass Gramm's legislation, affectionately known as the Citigroup Relief Act. Then, Rubin joined Citigroup's board. He received $126 million in compensation over the next eight years.

Despite receiving this enormous sum for his expertise, when all hell broke loose in 2008, Rubin denied knowing of the risks the corporation was taking and took no responsibility for the consequences of his management advice. After spearheading financial deregulation and promoting very questionable and risky practices, he did what any good corporate leader would do in that situation: He threw up his hands and said, "Who, me?" In his belated mea culpa, published in *Newsweek* on December 29, 2009, Rubin dutifully acknowledged that "the market-based model must be combined with strong and effective government, nationally and internationally, to deal with critical challenges that markets won't adequately address." Now he tells us.

Citigroup exemplifies the big American financial corporation perfectly. It merged in violation of the law, participated in a $300 million lobbying effort to remove restrictions, and then helped write the legislation that got it off the hook. Wonderfully deregulated, it flew high in the 2000s until the downturn. In November 2008, after four losing quarters, billions in write-downs, and a $45 billion infusion from the government, after laying off fifty-two thousand workers and paying its top guy $38 million, its

CEO announced, "The Company is entering 2009 in a strong position." Ta da!

In February 2000, Fed chairman Alan Greenspan became a cheerleader for derivative trading on Wall Street. "US laws impede [derivative] development," he testified to Congress. "Time is running out for us to modernize our regulation of financial markets before we lose them and the associated profits and employment opportunities to foreign jurisdictions that impose no such impediments."[3] Modernize? Did he say modernize? What he wanted was a return to the jungle, where his buddies and former partners would be free to rape and pillage; otherwise they might leave the United States and set up shop elsewhere. This is blackmail, nothing more, nothing less. If we don't bow to corruption, loosen legitimate regulations, and make the Federal Reserve Wall Street's private bank, some other country will.

Both Greenspan and then–Treasury secretary Larry Summers wanted to exclude derivatives from future regulation. They knew the kind of money there was to be made and didn't want anything cutting into those multibillion-dollar profits. After all, the investment bankers were their people before they joined the government and would be again. As head of the Senate Banking Committee, Senator Gramm took care of everything. He slipped an amendment entitled the Commodity Futures Modernization Act of 2000 (CMFA) into a big appropriations bill. Fortuitously, this legislation also contained the infamous "Enron loophole" that exempted that company from regulatory oversight. Gramm's wife, Wendy, formerly head of the Commodities Future Exchange, joined Enron's board of directors heading its *audit* committee, a position that would yield a seven-figure income for the Gramms before the company imploded, sending a few executives to jail and countless employees to the poorhouse.

Most people are familiar with the notion of commodities

trading—like gambling on the future price of corn or wheat crops. Derivatives are basically bets on just about anything—whether interest rates will go up or down, whether AIG will pay or default on a bond contract. You don't have to be a party to the deal to bet; you can gamble on anything. It defies common sense, but a single $50 tank of gasoline might support $750 to $1,000 in derivatives contracts. Most of these instruments are supported by . . . nothing.[4]

The ability to hedge against your own loan going bad creates serious "moral hazard." Think about it. If you can insure against losing, then why care how risky your bets are? Thanks to CFMA's deregulation, the market in derivatives took off in the nineties, as did irresponsible and corrupt lending practices.

Back in 1997, Brooksley Born chaired the Commodities Futures Trading Commission (CFTC); regulating derivatives was her responsibility. She recognized quickly that without careful oversight, derivative trading could put our whole economy at risk. In a PBS *Frontline* program, "The Warning," Born spoke candidly about her attempts to regulate the derivatives market and the opposition she encountered. "[As] chair of the CFTC, I became aware of how quickly the over-the-counter derivatives market was growing, how little any of the federal regulators knew about it. [T]here was no oversight . . . no regulation . . . enormous leverage was permitted, enormous borrowing. There was also little or no capital being put up as collateral." She listed her questions and concerns in a "concept paper" published in the *Federal Register*. Hoping for input from the financial industry, what she got instead was stonewalling and attacks on her character. "I was shocked that there was a strong negative reaction to merely asking questions about a market."

At the time, SEC Chairman Arthur Levitt served on President Clinton's Working Group on Financial Markets. Speaking about Born, he said, "I was told that she was irascible, difficult, stubborn, unreasonable." Throughout history, labeling people as crazy or histrionic has been a great way to sideline their efforts and, often, the truth. It is a very common tactic used against powerful women. Other Working Group principals, including Alan Greenspan and former Treasury secretary Robert Rubin, convinced Levitt that any regulation of the derivative market would create "financial turmoil, a conclusion he now believes was 'clearly a mistake.'"[5]

The PBS report documents this exchange. "I walk into Brooksley's office one day; the blood has drained from her face," says Michael Greenberger, a former top official at the CFTC. "She's hanging up the telephone; she says to me: 'That was [then–Undersecretary for International Affairs] Larry Summers. He says, You're going to cause the worst financial crisis since the end of World War Two. . . . [He says he has] thirteen bankers in his office who informed him of this. Stop, right away. No more.'"

Wall Street wanted to sideline Born and stifle her message. The White House economists obliged. Remember, these men were "the smartest guys in the room." Several of them are advising President Obama and still managing the economy. And you wonder why we can't seem to get effective regulations passed?

By March 2003, Warren Buffett was telling the BBC that these "complex financial instruments are time bombs. . . . Some derivatives contracts appear to have been *devised by madmen* . . . [they] pose a dangerous incentive for false accounting . . . [some] are the result of huge-scale fraud." He reminded viewers that derivatives trading in the energy market brought down Enron. He concluded by saying that "Berkshire Hathaway . . . is pulling out of the market, closing down [its] derivatives trading subsidiary." When the Oracle from Omaha speaks, it is usually worth a listen. Buffett is respected as an ethical businessman, but he's a very savvy trader. Good business, like good government, is what's good for America.

But the nation was on a roll. Our politicians were euphoric, and Born and Buffett were just party poopers. No matter how smart you were, opposition was unacceptable.

In *The Big Short: Inside the Doomsday Machine*, Michael Lewis reveals the role corrupt investment bankers played in creating and exploiting the crisis. He chronicles the adventures of hedge-fund manager Michael Burry, who made a fortune betting against the subprime mortgage bond market. Burry had no special insight; he simply read the mortgage bond prospectuses. By late 2004, lending standards were in the toilet. "A lot of people couldn't actually afford to pay their mortgages the old-fashioned way, and so the lenders were dreaming up new financial instruments to justify handing them new money . . . constantly degrading their own standards to grow loan volumes." Burry started betting against the industry, but he still couldn't understand why they were making such crappy deals.

Then Burry figured it out. The bankers didn't care who they loaned money to. They were flipping the mortgages to Goldman Sachs, Morgan Stanley, Wells Fargo, and the rest, where they were bundled together and quickly sold off. If the original borrowers defaulted, it was no longer their problem, and since the investment houses were betting on both sides, they didn't care either.

On November 5, 2005, the *Wall Street Journal* reported that relatively new adjustable-rate mortgages were defaulting at very high rates. Because these were *new* loans, this tells you that they were bad from the start. Rather than falling on hard times, this group of borrowers were unqualified from the get-go; they were never able to make the payments. Burry thought his ride was over. Surely lenders would clean up their act, and regulators would halt the practice.

Instead, the lending sped up. The investment bankers kept packaging and peddling this garbage, while increasing their own bets *against* the very products they were selling to their clients. They were making a fortune creating the deals, knowing the profits would be huge when it all collapsed.

While running Goldman Sachs, Henry Paulson securitized

billions in mortgages. By February 2006, when he became Bush's secretary of the Treasury, his company was already betting against those very deals. Paulson joined with Bush's SEC chairman, Christopher Cox, to call off the cops by dismantling the regulators' derivative review responsibilities. In April 2007, Fed Chairman Ben Bernanke said that the housing market was showing "signs of softening," but a "sharp slowdown" was unlikely. By June 2007, the subprime market had tanked. These guys want us to believe they didn't know what was happening? This doesn't just smell, it stinks to high heaven.

By June 2006, figures showed that "worldwide over-the-counter nominal derivatives" had grown by more than $72 *trillion* in the preceding six months. That 180-day increase was greater than the value of all such derivatives *on the entire planet* in 1999 when the deregulation legislation was passed.[6] By the time things crumbled in 2008, the over-the-counter derivatives market was estimated at over *$600 trillion*, and about 80 percent were *purely speculative instruments with no underlying assets to back them up.* That's about ninety thousand dollars of worthless paper for every person on Earth.[7]

As of March 2010, investment in these derivatives had returned to this astounding level. That's $600 trillion worth of nothing, and we're defending this as the future of global finance. Our financial rags are already betting on the next economic bubble, and you'd better believe that Wall Street has both sides covered. Responsible government regulations, independent supervising agencies, separation of investment banking from commercial institutions—we know what sort of measures are needed. We just don't have enough honest politicians in Washington to get such legislation passed.

Remember how some Republican pundits pitched this story? The crisis was caused by scheming buyers who got loans only after the Community Reinvestment Act (CRA) forced bankers to lower standards. It was the Democrats' fault, along with their big-government buddies at ACORN. CNBC's anchor Rick Santelli became a household name after spewing this argument while jumping around on the floor of the Stock Exchange. He was still repeating it well into 2010. It was great political fodder and helped energize the Tea Party movement.

If the CRA was the reason for the economic meltdown, I'd be on it like a rash, but rather than indulge in partisan finger-pointing, I prefer to review the evidence and figure out the real causes. I've concluded that the subprime crash had virtually nothing to do with the CRA. Don't take my word for it: You decide.

The CRA was created in the 1970s to stop discrimination and "redlining" by banks, a practice of refusing to loan to *qualified* buyers in poor neighborhoods. In 2008, the Federal Reserve examined whether the CRA affected the subprime crisis. According to Federal Reserve governor Randall Kroszner, "Only 6% of all the [subprime] loans were extended by CRA-covered lenders to lower-income borrowers or neighborhoods. . . . These studies found that lending to lower-income individuals and communities has been nearly as profitable and performed similarly to other types of lending done by CRA-covered institutions. Thus, the long-term evidence shows that the CRA has not pushed banks into extending loans that perform out of line with their traditional businesses . . . [this] makes it hard to imagine how this law could have contributed in any meaningful way to the current subprime crisis." The subprime loans made by Warren Buffett's Clayton Homes division were also performing normally, with delinquencies in the low single digits. He wasn't pushing for artificially high returns so he didn't need to churn out loans to unqualified buyers. It was pressure from Wall Street and the grand fees the originating banks were raking in that pushed lending standards lower.

Here's where Freddie Mac and Fannie Mae come in; two other

favored culprits in the GOP's scenario. I'm all for completely privatizing or eliminating these hybrid institutions, because I don't think our government should be in the home-buying business (a role that originated with Herbert Hoover in the 1920s). But to make a very long story short, this is yet another tale of collusion between government and Wall Street, and both groups are culpable.

Freddie Mac and Fannie Mae are "quasigovernmental agencies." They operate like private companies but have implicit guarantees from the government to back their plays. They are clearly "too big to fail." While these government-sponsored enterprises (GSEs) were *big* players and share responsibility for its magnitude, they did not *cause* the crisis.

All you have to do is look at the timelines and the numbers. By 2004, Fannie Mae had lost over half its loan-reselling business to Wall Street. Some of the big lenders were calling the GSEs irrelevant in the housing boom. Big shareholders in the GSEs were unhappy with their investment returns; other lenders were making much more money.

That year, the new head of Fannie Mae, Daniel H. Mudd, met with Countrywide Financial, then the nation's largest mortgage lender (and a prime culprit in the crisis). Countrywide sold more loans to Fannie Mae than anyone else. Its CEO, Angelo R. Mozilo, "threatened to upend their partnership unless Fannie started buying Countrywide's riskier loans [saying] that Countrywide had other options. . . . Firms like Bear Stearns, Lehman Brothers and Goldman Sachs had started bundling home loans and selling them to investors—bypassing Fannie and dealing with Countrywide directly. 'You're becoming irrelevant,' Mr. Mozilo told Mr. Mudd. . . . 'You need us more than we need you, and if you don't take these loans, you'll find you can lose much more.'"[8]

Given the quality of mortgages being created by lenders, the GSEs had to lower their standards to accept them. Before 2003, none of the GSE-purchased loans were "interest only"; by 2007, one-quarter of them were of this type. Yet reports show that the real damage came from adjustable-rate mortgages made to more affluent buyers.

On February 23, 2004, Fed chair Alan Greenspan gave a speech to the Credit Union National Association. He downplayed the growing American debt and touted ways to lend to people whose credit might not support a traditional mortgage. "American consumers might benefit if lenders provided greater mortgage product alternatives to the traditional fixed-rate mortgage. To the degree that households are driven by fears of payment shocks but are willing to manage their own interest rate risks, the traditional fixed-rate mortgage may be an expensive method of financing a home."

Just as in the 1920s, the mission was to get more consumers to buy homes. The real estate, construction, and investment banking industries were desperate to tap less-qualified buyers, and Greenspan was going to help them out. Time and again, our leaders ignore the end game—when debtors crash and burn. Just keep those plates spinning and hope they don't fall on your watch. Even if they do, your thankful contributors will have you covered.

The adjustable-rate mortgage, a creature designed as part of the S&L deregulation in the early eighties, received Greenspan's stamp of approval. So the GSEs bought even more of these loans. They became toxic to both prime and subprime buyers, and a major cause of Fannie's and Freddie's problems. According to an investigation by *Barron's*, the notion that the GSEs got into trouble because they had to buy loans to meet required affordable-housing targets was "more than disingenuous." Their major credit losses came from "Alt-A mortgages [riskier than prime loans but not subprime] that the agencies imprudently bought or guaranteed in recent years *to boost their market share*," mortgages made to speculators "in the ex-urbs of Las Vegas or Los Angeles, not to low-income folks in the inner cities."[9]

*Barron's* is no liberal rag; it is a Wall Street investment Bible. It concluded that the GSEs were responding to pressures from their big investors—hedge fund managers, Wall Street companies, and pension funds—to take more risk and increase their profits. Their CEOs were happy to comply. Higher revenues meant bigger bonuses. Their implicit government guarantees and power in the market ensured they would have a big impact on the mortgage crisis, but it was the push to increase profits and boost stock prices that turned their portfolios toxic in 2006—not some liberal mandate that they sell more houses to unqualified poor folk. By 2007 the GSEs reinstituted tougher standards, but the damage was done.

Did GSE purchases of subprime mortgage securities sustain bad lending practices? Yes. Did they lower their own lending standards to do this? Yes. Did their implicit government guarantees create moral hazard in lenders? Yes. Did they *cause* the financial crisis? No.

It is worth noting that other developed nations with no comparable public/private lenders experienced the same housing boom and bust. Our GSEs exacerbated the problem late in the game, but it was the Wall Street gurus and their international compadres who made the mess.

The reasons for our current crisis are clear. Repeat after me: deregulation with lax supervision, low interest rates, cheap credit, asset speculation, pursuit of bigger risk for higher returns, and the big bankers' faith that the government would bail them out if they crashed. The only variation from other historical financial crises is the deadly new twist—the derivative. Suddenly there are a lot of debts out there with no underlying hard assets to cover them.

Former Fed chair Paul Volcker explained this game changer. We moved "from a commercial bank-centered, highly regulated financial system, to an enormously more complicated and highly engineered system. Today, much of the financial intermediation takes place in markets beyond effective official oversight and supervision, all enveloped in unknown trillions of derivative instruments."

When Henry Paulson defended the Bear Stearns bailout to Congress in April 2008, he said it was necessary to prevent "severe damage to the U.S. economy and global financial system. . . . Stock prices may have plunged, and the resulting turmoil would have worsened the existing credit crunch by further lowering home prices and drying up credit for homeowners and businesses."[10] All this happened anyway, but his comments are an admission that our policies were so out of whack that the failure of a single investment house might bring the most powerful nation on the planet to its knees. And we're dithering over whether to regulate these guys?

In opposing needed reforms, Republicans are making the same arguments that got us into this mess in the first place. Government regulation is bad; deregulation is good. Big corporations can monitor themselves. Government officials are incompetent; CEOs can be trusted. What is good for Wall Street is good for Main Street. And on it goes. Either no one in the GOP does their homework, or they're simply lying to us.

This crisis should confirm a few things once and for all. Take notes. Transnational financial companies (the big guys on Wall Street) are American in name only. The vast majority of funds held by Wall Street "bankers" are *not* loaned to real Americans or U.S. businesses to expand operations. They go into these derivatives and currency trading and into electronic paper that floats between computers until someone cashes in—and that always includes the traders. You should know that Wall Street pays out between 50 and 60 percent of its generated revenue to employees as compensation. They get all the benefits of a big public company but continue to operate like private fiefdoms.

Remember how companies used to earn the privilege of incorporation by providing a valuable service? Originally, Wall Street investment banks were established to locate and provide capital for major ventures. Today, that function has almost disappeared. At

Goldman Sachs, "Trading and investing for the firm's account produced 76 percent of revenue [in 2009]. *Investment banking, which raises capital for productive enterprise, accounted for a mere 11 percent.* Other than that, it could have been a hedge fund."[11]

Essentially, Wall Street is chasing short-term profits through trading and speculation. It then plows those profits into annual bonuses. It couldn't care less about meaningful growth in our domestic economy or the well-being of American citizens. *These guys are not banks.* They are traders and gamblers that our lawmakers and regulators have disguised as responsible lenders.

Americans are consumption machines. The more we buy, especially as wages remain stagnant or fall, the more we must borrow. We still manufacture something in this country—debt, and this product is just fodder for the international traders.

Those lower rates and better services we were promised with deregulation? Nope; the worse things have gotten, the higher our costs have climbed. These "bankers" are making record profits, yet check out the interest rates on our credit cards. First Premier issued a new card in 2009 for those with really poor credit. They don't care if you can pay it back; they got the laws changed so this debt is almost impossible to discharge in bankruptcy. The new card had a minimum annual fee of $256 for a credit line of $250. When new laws invalidated that charge, First Premier simply lowered the fee to $75 and jacked annual interest rates from 9.9 to 79.9 percent. This is not a legitimate lender; it is a loan shark.

The postgame analysis continues, with the government blaming the traders, and the traders blaming the government. U.S. Treasury Secretary Timothy F. Geithner has singled out the lack of integrity and good judgment in our top CEOs, saying, "Regulation cannot produce integrity, foresight or judgment in those responsible for managing these institutions."[12] Now for the corporate perspective: Berkshire Hathaway vice chairman Charlie Munger targets the regulators: "When the tiger gets out and starts creating damage, it's insane to blame the tiger, it's the idiot tiger keeper" we should blame.[13] Wall Street and its favored politicians gutted the supervisory agencies, the credit rating agencies were paid off, yet somehow when it all collapsed, the government was entirely at fault.

These are two very bright, very experienced men. One blames Wall Street integrity, the other, failed government oversight. Both are right. This is why the partisan nonsense on Capitol Hill drives me crazy. Keep us distracted and divided—and nothing will change.

Remember the essential questions at the beginning of this chapter: Do policies achieve their stated goals, and do the results ultimately benefit the nation as a whole? The last thirty years of market fundamentalism were supposed to encourage competition, improve services, reduce consumer costs, and increase revenues despite the big subsidies and tax cuts for those at the top. All boats would rise in a buoyant economy. Well, the admirals are still on deck bellowing "Stay the course" while the rest of us drown. These guys no longer need American workers and consumers to man the ship.

Hamilton's corporatism can be a powerful asset when properly checked, but unleashed, it devours with little discrimination. Like the scorpion, such is its nature. The men and women who rule these institutions are there to maximize short-term profits, period. Regardless of their personal ethics, time and again, the lure of power and money win out.

We must heed the words of Jefferson and Smith. We must reject ideological propaganda and examine the facts. We must relearn the lessons that our own history provides. The Founders entrusted this nation and its government to the people. If we choose to remain gullible and ignorant, preferring partisan speeches at flag-waving rallies to the cold, hard truth, then we'll get what we deserve—a Republic in name only.

We are not helpless. We still have the ability to read, learn, and think for ourselves. We have the right to petition our government, to peacefully assemble and to make our voices heard. We still have a democracy on Election Day. The cure for these problems is not a socialist takeover, but a rational understanding of the economic system that has replaced American capitalism and the steps needed to pursue the democratic market economy once envisioned for this extraordinary Republic.

# VIII.

## *Mapping Our Economic Future*

There's class warfare, all right. But it's my class, the rich class, that's making war, and we're winning.

—*Warren Buffett, billionaire investor*

It is time to rethink our relationship with modern capitalism. As originally imagined, it was the perfect economic system for a free nation. All of the values we cherish—liberty, opportunity, self-determination, and true independence—were supported and enhanced by Adam Smith's theories. Each citizen could compete fairly in a system that, for the most part, would leave him or her alone to pursue personal ambitions. However, like Thomas Jefferson's perfect democracy, this ideal works best on a small scale. He and Smith recognized what would happen as power and wealth combined.

Industrialization, economies of scale, increased productivity—we applaud all of these revolutionary developments. However, they changed the game dramatically. The worker became a disposable commodity rather than a respected, integral part of society. This is not a prolabor lament, just an economic reality. Corporations acquired more and more power through the courts and legislatures. With economic, legal, and political advantages, they were able to rig the playing field—moving the country further away from free market ideals. Globalization so expanded the corporate reach that these huge companies can go elsewhere for their workers and profits. At the height of the financial crisis, the U.S. transnational corporations were posting record returns even as American citizens were cutting up their credit cards and applying for unemployment benefits.

Our Congress is so beholden to the campaign money from these corporations that *it will not act* to balance the inequities. Instead, politicians continue to favor this sector as big businesses dismantle our domestic economy, abuse America's human and natural resources at taxpayers' expense, and expand control over essential services only to raise rates and lower performance. We have become so brainwashed that any objection is branded as a call for class warfare or an attack on individual liberty and free market capitalism. When we accept this rhetoric, despite decades of clear empirical evidence, we are abdicating the well-being of our people and our nation to a tiny group of the political and commercial elite.

The economic rescue that began with Bush in 2008 was necessary to stabilize our financial system and auto industry. We had to save them because we'd given them the keys to our economic well-being; it was that or another Great Depression. Today, it looks like the Bush/Obama TARP program was a relative success. We may be out some $50 billion, but that's a small price to pay, considering the alternative. Despite cries of socialism, our government never took over private industries, but instead, ensured that many average Americans kept working in jobs that would have vanished without the assistance.

Where the government went wrong was failing to use stimulus money to invest in America. Handouts to big business are not the same as rebuilding our domestic economy. Alexander Hamilton knew that creating infrastructure and investing in our future would make money for everyone. Today, with interest rates at nearly zero, low labor costs, and the construction industry with all its suppliers scrambling for work, we should be pouring stimulus dollars into our schools, roads, and bridges. We should be building the new energy grid and sending wireless technology into every corner of the land. These are the public investments that will create a platform for entrepreneurs and domestic businesses to grow and prosper; these are the measures that will produce big returns for all Americans.

Not only is the timing right, but without this investment, our future is in peril. A bipartisan report issued in October 2010 concluded that America's "rapidly decaying and woefully underfunded transportation system will undermine [our] status in the global economy . . . and lead to a steady erosion of the social and economic foundations for American prosperity in the long run."[1] Major investment in our country's infrastructure is essential if we are to remain competitive.

Yet here we are, with an enormous deficit, defending tax cuts for the top 1 percent of the country as our cities and towns close up shop. Today, the divide between rich and poor—actually between the top 10 percent and the rest of the country—is greater than it has ever been. In the midst of a horrific downturn, the upper tier continues to rake in money; not on merit (which would be laudable) but thanks to *special treatment*, based on the specious argument that they are responsible for jobs and investments in America, that they somehow take care of the rest of us. This is patently false.

Cut taxes on the rich (individuals, corporations, capital gains, and so on) and this money will be reinvested at home, so the argument goes. This theory became a mainstay for Reagan in the 1980s, but it didn't happen. Just look at the numbers. Without the additional tax revenue, the government deficit ballooned. The rich reinvested about a third of their tax savings, but much of this went overseas or into the new world of paper assets. These investors were leaving the United States while encouraging the rest of us to use our new credit cards and spend like crazy on all those cheap products from China. Ordinary citizens became debt-producing machines in the new profit schemes devised by and for the rich.

In the 2000s, the Bush tax cuts again rewarded those at the top, and the same thing occurred at an accelerated pace. This money *did not* go back into the development of America's domestic economy but was spent on more toys or invested overseas, so there was nothing to trickle down. Ordinary Americans didn't notice because they were riding high on cheap credit until the house of cards collapsed.

One thing we must take from Reagan's tax policies was his belief that *there should be equal taxes on income from wealth and income from work*. His Tax Reform Act of 1986 made the rate on long-term capital gains the same as that on wages and salaries. He knew then what we're relearning now, that the justification for a lower tax rate on long-term gains is based on a lie. The claim that investment in the stock market drives investment in new businesses and new jobs *in America* is not true.

Today, Republicans are arguing for a complete elimination of capital gains taxes. Just who are they representing? Wealthy investors can pour money into derivatives or multinational corporations and pocket most of the profits. There is no incentive to invest those profits in American businesses that employ American workers and create American consumers who can actually buy stuff and keep our domestic engine operating.

Here's the truth. The higher the capital gains and corporate tax, the more incentive there is to reinvest profits because that money then becomes *a tax deduction*. Remember, economic growth in this country from the mid-1950s to sixties was tremendous, yet the upper tax rate exceeded 60 percent throughout this period. It reached 91 percent during the Eisenhower administration. I'm not advocating such a rate, but we must learn the lessons of history and economics.

Ah, but then everyone will leave America and move overseas, the politicians tell us. Good Lord, we've been using the tax code as a political payoff for years. How about we use it to encourage growth at home? If you want to foster domestic innovation and the small business community, that's easy. Target the tax breaks to these groups and their investors. Help entrepreneurs. Encourage research and development. Reward job creation in America. All other long-term gains should be taxed the same as wages, just as Reagan insisted.

Experts are finally acknowledging what has been happening for years—that corporate profits no longer have much to do with the betterment of the lives of most citizens in this country. Some economists claim that the recession ended in 2009 because the stock market turned around and profits went up. But those numbers are as phony as the paper our financial gurus have been churning out. They show that the banks have been borrowing from taxpayers at zero percent. They've traded with this money, made profits for their own accounts, and recorded "revenue growth." Foreign divisions of American corporations are moving ahead. Troubled companies are being scooped up by private equity firms, downsized, and sold for parts, only after they've been leveraged with unsustainable debts so the investors make every buck they can before peddling the carcasses. Our GDP looks better and stock prices have gone up, but for about 95 percent of the population, nothing has changed.

For all you budding capitalists out there, do you think that you could show a profit if you were handed free money, and then were allowed to buy and sell lots of stuff and pocket the proceeds? If you lose money, the government—the taxpayers—will eat the losses and bail you out. Even a third-grader could get rich under this scheme. But a third-grader can't do this . . . only the really big guys get to play. This is what passes for free enterprise in corporate America today.

Remember the political promises that America would replace manufacturing jobs with exciting new knowledge sector jobs? Where did these people get the idea that we had an education system that could train such workers or that somehow knowledge jobs wouldn't leave as quickly as manufacturing jobs? At least with the latter, you have to build facilities, buy a lot of equipment, and spend time and money to get new plants up and running. With white-collar positions, a computer and maybe a desk is all that's required. An employee can be shipped overseas for the cost of a plane ticket, but nowadays, there are educated workers in China and India ready to take those jobs.

Other countries are taking advantage of our economic situation. The Chinese aren't stupid. They're making sweet deals to get our manufacturers over there, and then they're requiring the companies to hand over their research and proprietary information. While Google appears to be taking a stand and choosing to leave rather than give up its patented information, some believe that the Chinese have already hacked the knowledge they need to expand their own national search engine, which has already cornered more than 60 percent of its market.

The Chinese know a country cannot survive if it doesn't have a manufacturing base. They've brought our businesses over there to obtain what they need to go it alone. Even some of our financial corporations are finding themselves cut out of deals. Why pay for the milk if you can get the cow for free? But unlike the Chinese, our CEOs think only short-term. They are willing to blow our future for an uptick in their stock price or improvement in the next quarter's returns. They're selling out our financial future for those easy overseas profits.

Some people argue that America is still the land of innovation and point to our extraordinary research universities as proof. You'd better check out the home countries of those graduate students and patent holders. Our immigration welcome mat for these people has been rolled up. They're coming here to learn and then taking that American education overseas. Selfishly, I should add that even reporters' jobs have been leaving. They're writing our news stories in India.

"Who is against jobs in the United States? The big banks, Wall Street, the Council on Foreign Relations, the Business Roundtable, the United States Chamber of Commerce, the National Retail Federation, Corporate America, the President of the United States, Congress of the United States. Everyone is crying for jobs, but no one seems to understand why there aren't any." Former senator Fritz Hollings wrote this in January 2010, lamenting the offshoring of American jobs. He included some pretty alarming poll results. "The Council on Foreign Relations ought to be renamed the Council on Making Money. A recent Pew poll reported fully 85 percent of Americans said that protecting U.S. jobs should be a top foreign policy priority. But only 21 percent of the Council on Foreign Relations agrees. Financial interests organized the Business Roundtable to continue off-shore investment and profit. The local Chamber is for Main Street America, but Tom Donahue and the United States Chamber have sold out to the financial interests and oppose jobs and producing in the United States . . . Senator Byron Dorgan of North Dakota long ago tried to allocate the tax incentive for foreign jobs and production to domestic jobs and production. The Business Roundtable and the U.S. Chamber fought it like a tiger and killed it."[2]

I am no economist, but this scenario doesn't make sense to me. Large multinational corporations with little allegiance to the United States are flagged offshore. They earn enormous profits and plug them back into overseas operations where they're not taxed by the United States. They provide cheap products to Americans who can afford little more. Consumerism is the mantra; insidious marketing is everywhere, so we go further into debt. When we literally can't take on any more, the banks and lenders come up with crazy instruments, no-asset loans or 79.9 percent credit cards, to keep us buying. Wages have been flat for decades and jobs continue to disappear; the GDP reflects the well-being of these companies rather than the nation or its people. Not only are our production facilities leaving the country, but the innovations and new manufacturing techniques are occurring overseas. In this country, most of our research is handled by foreigners who then take their training back home. Industries necessary for our national security are long gone. We've moved from an agricultural- to industrial- to technological- then service- and now a debt-based economy. With every economic dip or terrorist attack, we're told to go shopping. Until the '08 recession, Americans had forgotten how to save, and already we're increasing our consumption again even though the jobs haven't returned. Our politicians encourage this. The failure to consume at a high level means a falling GDP, and they know that most voters still believe this reflects American prosperity.

Consumption as the only means to grow an economy makes no sense. A nation must be founded on more than the "eating up" of goods and services, particularly as we confront the reality of resource scarcity and environmental degradation. But setting aside those minor concerns, we're impoverishing the very people expected to do all that consuming. It is the poor and middle classes that spend most of their income every month. Without jobs that deliver a living wage to people who then can service their debts and have a little money left over for retirement, there is no foundation for our consumption economy. Even Wal-Mart is blaming lackluster U.S. revenues on the fact that their customers cannot afford to shop there. We're impoverishing America's citizens—all to profit the transnational corporations.

If this wasn't bad enough, our financial institutions have shown their true nature. The rampant fraud and corruption in our financial industry is staggering, as it is in other industries like health insurance and oil and mining. Pick your category. They are all being investigated for serious illegal conduct. This behavior by our captains of industry has been fostered for decades by government officials who deregulated their institutions, legislated loopholes, and neutered regulatory agencies while selling these "innovations" as free market capitalism and the American way.

Not surprisingly, when technologies emerge that level the economic and political playing field, there is a mad scramble by the global elite to control such tools and maintain their advantage. In a show of true democracy and capitalism, average citizens now use the Internet to sidestep corporate and government gatekeepers and market their products and ideas to the world. As a result, there is a major push by corporations to control access to this powerful thoroughfare.

Just as corporations were allowed to purchase most of the public airwaves for their television and radio programming, they now seek to own the broadband pipeline through which all wireless communications flow. While claiming that they want to profit only by building and managing the wireless infrastructure, the big telecoms are spending millions to oppose "net neutrality" and thereby maintain the right to control what sort of content passes through their portals.

Imagine granting a company the right to build and maintain all bridges from a remote island to the mainland. In exchange for its investment, the corporation will profit by charging a toll to everyone who crosses over. One day, it decides to let those who can pay more go to the head of the line. Another day, it decides too many kids are crossing and limit the number of children allowed to pass each day. Then, it targets certain companies that truck materials to its competitors by doubling its tolls and allowing those vehicles to cross only after midnight. Finally, it refuses to build additional bridges to handle the traffic. Those who can't pay enough or are not approved for passage are out of luck. You can see how controlling the broadband pipeline becomes a way to manipulate competition and shape—or censor—the information that passes through it.

Would the real patriots who believe in the Constitution, in democracy, and in the Republic please stand up? It is so difficult to challenge what are portrayed as fundamental principles of American democracy—capitalism, free enterprise—without losing an audience. Yet as long as the real culprits can wave the flag and distract us from their subversive behavior, we lose. As long as we value ideology and partisanship over truth, we lose. The liars exist on both sides of the political aisle and throughout the world of high finance and corporate America.

Capitalism is not a democratic institution. It is an economic term of art. Innovation and entrepreneurship flourished long before this philosophy was articulated. Today, Smith's ideals, even Hamilton's nation-centered mercantilism, have been replaced by an economic system serving multinational goliaths residing in the global arena. Yet we defend this evolution into corporatism with the same patriotic fervor we use to defend the Republic itself.

Many conservative and libertarian economic icons have been telling the truth for generations. Yet they are described as defenders of pure laissez-faire economics time and again. I guess the tactic is safe if no one actually reads their writings. In *Wealth of Nations*, Adam Smith wrote about prosperity, freedom, and initiative, but he argued that these values were threatened by the marriage of the wealthy capitalists and government. While Friedrich von Hayek's *The Road to Serfdom* challenged socialist central planning, it is no ringing endorsement of unregulated capitalism. Hayek supported all sorts of government intervention in areas where private enterprise doesn't work. He discussed the reality of imperfect knowledge in the markets that capitalists exploit to commit fraud and deceit. He described the need for government oversight and regulation and, heaven forbid, he even said, "The preservation of competition is not incompatible with an extensive system of [government] social services." Von Mises, Milton Friedman, and the newer converts like Alan Greenspan also provide a much more nuanced balancing of economic, social, and governmental issues than conservative ideologues will admit.

In 1947, as fears of communism clouded our thinking, the FBI branded *It's a Wonderful Life* a subversive film. Triumph of the little banker, George Bailey, over the great capitalist was a communist message—political propaganda that attacked wealth and the profit motive. Even *Mr. Smith Goes to Washington* was deemed socialism in disguise. What a difference a few decades can make, as now these films are beloved and iconic American stories. It is time that we defend again the small business owner and the honest politician as true heroes.

As of now, they've become merely pawns in a much larger enterprise. It is maddening to listen as activists rail against big business or government without understanding that the danger lies in the *union* of these giants. Conservatives, liberals, Tea Partiers—all of us must understand this basic reality before advocating solutions. More policies promoting allegedly free markets and lax regulation for these multinational corporations are nightmarish in their consequences. More government control by those who are bought and paid for by the very institutions they're designed to monitor is equally ridiculous. More guarantees that the taxpayer will foot the bill by socializing risk and privatizing reward is outrageous.

The principles of free enterprise have been corrupted by behemoth corporations that *own* many elected officials. As bankers and lobbyists make record sums, as taxpayer dollars flood Wall Street accounts, as too big to fail becomes an excuse for ditching the rules mere mortals must observe, the American people must recognize that their idealistic view of capitalism and business in this country has been crushed by the very elected officials who proclaim allegiance to traditional conservative principles. It is a sham.

Sadly, every criticism of the ethics, shady dealing, and manipulation by corporations can be applied to government and our political process. Both sides of this marriage must be subjected to reform for real change to occur. Thanks to the Supreme Court ruling in *Citizens United* v. *FEC*, our government is now for sale to the highest bidder, and these transnational corporations are *not* lobbying for pro-American policies. The U.S. Chamber of Commerce, dominated by huge corporate interests, collects dues from its branches in other countries, such as Dubai, Russia, India, and China. It uses that money in political attack ads that oppose things like tax relief for businesses that hire locally rather than choosing to outsource jobs.

Enough with the phony rhetoric and flag waving by those who simultaneously stab Main Street in the back. Enough from politicians who whitewash our enormous problems with weak reforms. Enough with the revolving door between regulatory agencies, government offices, and corporate headquarters.

Conservatives should be screaming their support for reform as our transnational economic system disavows political and corporate integrity, destroys personal liberty, ensures the growth of government, and endangers our national security. Liberals should be outraged at the subsidizing of corporate wealth, the corruption of our electoral process, and the destruction of the middle class. Do you see how these interests overlap? When we really examine the problems, there is no red or blue. There is no difference in what people want or need. We must acknowledge this, because the only power still capable of countering a united corporate America and federal government is the people themselves—an informed, united citizenry willing to ditch phony ideology and reclaim their country.

American capitalism was never a free enterprise system, and today, it is hard to call it American. Big corporations make important contributions to our nation and the world. Demonizing them is *not* my intent. However, I do hope I've debunked the notion that these institutions represent true American capitalism or that their interests and operations should be central to our economic and political security.

The real fuel in our economic engine is the entrepreneur and small business owner. They create most new jobs, support local communities, and sustain the American consumer, yet they are virtually ignored by the politicians in Washington. If encouraging free market capitalism is a worthy goal, here is where to begin.

The interests of this nation and her people are an essential part of the free market equation. Fair regulation and substantive reform of our economic system must proceed without further delay.

IX.

## Health Care for Sale

With the possible exception of the investment bankers and defense contractors, there are no more powerful corporatists in America than those who rule the health care and pharmaceutical oligopolies. They have done a masterful job of falsely framing the health care debate as a struggle between individual liberty and government mandates, between quality care and bureaucratic rationing, and between free market capitalism and an alleged socialist threat to dismantle what they claim is the finest health care system in the world.

The real culprit is being swept under the rug. A nation's health care system cannot operate simply to maximize short-term profits. It should be structured as a long-term investment in our human infrastructure, an investment that provides economic and social returns for every American. This is not a plug for a government takeover or a threat to eliminate fair returns on good investments in the private health care marketplace. Instead, it is a request to rethink the corporatist business model that is used now by doctors and hospitals as well as the insurance and drug industries.

Here's the reality: The U.S. health care system ranks number one in cost but not in quality. We spend at least 50 percent more per person and almost 50 percent more of our GDP on health care than the next most costly nation, yet when compared to seventeen wealthy industrialized countries, we rank last in overall health care performance. In certain critical categories, such as global life expectancy and infant mortality, America trails many Third World nations.[1]

In fact, our health care facilities can be dangerous places. In a twenty-six-nation study, the United States had the third-highest number of *preventable* medical errors. More than two hundred thousand Americans die annually from outright mistakes such as unnecessary surgery, medication errors, and hospital infections. (Some reports conclude that the number is closer to half a million people.) Only heart disease and cancer kill more of our citizens each year, and according to *The Wall Street Journal*, injury and death from preventable errors cost the U.S. economy at least $19.5 billion in 2008, about half of this in direct health care costs.

The Congressional Budget Office concluded that the 2010 "Obamacare" legislation will slow the rate of growth in health care costs over the next decade, but it's hard to see how this is going to happen. Just take a look at the numbers. In the last decade, average health costs per family have more than doubled and projections show that this upward trend will continue. Medicare and Medicaid already cost 50 percent more than Congress appropriates for all other domestic agencies, and in 2011, the first baby boomers turned sixty-five. Our population is living longer, and as we age, more expensive drugs and technologies are used to prolong life. Our children and young adults are suffering more illnesses at earlier ages, exacerbated by the obesity epidemic. Currently, some twenty-six million young Americans between the ages of seventeen and twenty-four can't meet minimum military standards of physical fitness (which have been lowered to attract recruits). Collectively, our population is a health care disaster, thanks in large part to our poor diet, sedentary lifestyle, increased exposure to chemicals and toxins, and persistent overmedicating. By 2020, one of every five dollars spent in the United States will go to health care.

This system is bankrupting the nation morally, financially, and physically. Until we address the core issues—why our costs are so high, why our outcomes are so poor and why, as a nation, we're in such bad shape—there can be no meaningful reform. The answers lie in a democratic balancing of interests, the application of true capitalist principles and an informed electorate willing to accept some personal responsibility to reverse this national crisis.

Throughout the health care debate in 2009 and 2010, the real fight on Capitol Hill was over who pays—and who profits. The Republicans knew they couldn't win if our system was scrutinized under true capitalist principles, so they made it a debate about the role of government. Republican wordsmith and pollster Frank Luntz issued talking points for GOP party members, telling them to use words like "bureaucrats" and "Washington," not terms like "the free market" or "competition." People "are deathly afraid that a government takeover [one of his catchphrases] will lower their quality of care—so they are extremely receptive to the anti-Washington approach. It's not an *economic* issue. It's a *bureaucratic* issue."[2]

This is blatantly false. Unless you're paying in cash, there are always bureaucrats involved; only the motives differ. The private insurance gatekeepers make decisions to maximize profits while the government employees are charged with holding down taxpayer costs. The debate is all about economics; it's all about the money.

Despite the common assertion that Obamacare is a socialist takeover of the system, big business won almost every scrimmage in the legislative battle. A handful of private corporations still dominate the insurance marketplace and remain exempt from antitrust laws. They have millions of new customers, thanks to the requirement that everyone have basic coverage. Government subsidies will help low-income purchasers and small businesses write those checks to Aetna, United Health Care, and the other big insurers. The drug companies are still protected from overseas imports and

can freely jack up prices to counter any government-mandated rebates. And sure enough, despite kicking and screaming about the
legislation, these industries posted record profits in 2010 and are
on target to beat those numbers in 2011.

I was surprised when Republicans objected to basic mandatory
insurance in Obama's health care bill, because they've pushed the
idea since Nixon's day. George H. W. Bush picked it up, as did the
conservative Heritage Foundation in 1989 and 1993. Mitt Romney
made it the centerpiece of his reforms in Massachusetts. "Someone
has to pay for the health care that must, by law, be provided: Either
the individual pays or the taxpayers pay." He decided—no free ride
on the government; it's the individual's responsibility.[3]

But after passage of Obamacare, Sen. Orrin Hatch (R-UT)
said, "Congress has never crossed the line between regulating what
people choose to do and ordering them to do it. . . . The difference
between regulating and requiring is liberty." I guess the definition
of liberty has changed since Hatch and nineteen other Republican
senators, including Chuck Grassley, Robert Bennett, and Christopher Bond, cosponsored 1993 legislation, Senate Bill 1770, that
featured an individual mandate: Subtitle F, Universal Coverage.
This required each citizen or lawful permanent resident to be covered under a qualified health plan or equivalent health care program by January 1, 2005, complete with government vouchers for
those who couldn't pay the costs. That Republican bill and the current law have other similarities: Both call for purchasing pools and
standardized insurance plans; both call for a ban on insurers' denying coverage or raising premiums due to preexisting conditions;
both even call for increased federal research into the effectiveness
of medical treatments.

Senator Charles Grassley told Fox News in June 2009 that "ev-
erybody has some health insurance costs, and if you aren't insured,
there's no free lunch. . . . I believe that there is a bipartisan consen-

sus to have individual mandates." But by September of that year, he had received the Republican talking points and told Fox, "I'm very reluctant to go along with an individual mandate." There is only one reason for his 180-degree turn. In Grassley's political career, three of his four top contributors, by category, are in the health care business: health professionals, the insurance industry, and pharmaceuticals/health products.[4] The big guns issued his marching orders, and immediately he abandoned a position he'd defended for at least sixteen years.

Newt Gingrich has described Obamacare as "the biggest threat to the American way of life since the 1850s when the country was heading for civil war."[5] Yet in 2007, he was saying, "Citizens should not be able to cheat their neighbors by not buying insurance, particularly when they can afford it, and expect others to pay for their care when they need it."[6]

Echoing other rational suggestions, Gingrich has suggested policies to mandate exercise at school and prohibit unhealthy food choices in student cafeterias and vending machines. He proposed that the government subsidize fruits and vegetables in poor neighborhood grocery stores, build bike paths and parks and pay for recreational programs. He has stated emphatically, "We should eliminate any financial incentive to do any test, treatment or therapy that does not directly benefit the patient or add value to the care process."[7] These proposals are excellent—but I'm betting you'll hear none of this as Newt campaigns for president in 2012!

Our current health care system is disease-based rather than wellness-based. Treating disease with drugs and surgeries rather than preventing illness or catching problems early is the primary focus and a major cost inflator. Any other business that waited for things to break down, then used repeated temporary patches to repair equipment, would go broke in a hurry.

Doctors and hospitals drive profits by billing for each and every service, rather than outcomes. When you take your car in for repairs, you don't pay to use the service bay or for each mechanic that tinkers with the engine. You get an overall estimate, then pay for parts and labor and usually get a warranty in return. Of course, a responsible car owner will schedule regular tune-ups, check the tires, change the oil, and use recommended fuel to get the most mileage out of the vehicle. The analogy is imperfect, but you get the idea.

Insurance companies are exempt from antitrust laws and operate as corporate monopolies. They actively suppress competition in the marketplace while designing coverage to avoid risk rather than provide comprehensive insurance. The medical profession is a monopoly as well. Doctors purposefully restrict the number of students entering medical school to control supply and thus limit competition, elevating the cost of services. Similarly, the AMA wants states to retain control of the licensing of doctors. Currently, an MD licensed in one state cannot treat patients in another, nor can a clinic send X-rays to a radiologist across state lines. This is all about inhibiting competition.

The uninsured and underinsured are driving prices higher for all consumers. Employers and insured patients do not have enough skin in the game; with tax breaks and subsidies for most expenses, there are few personal and business incentives to cut costs. Selfishly, you should applaud the individual mandates and insist that everyone in this country have affordable insurance for basic medical care. Right now, those without coverage put off care until a crisis occurs, at which time the cost of treatment is very high. The uninsured pay for about one-third of their own medical costs. Government programs paid for by taxpayers and charities (again, taxpayer dollars) pick up another third of this tab, and the remaining amount, "uncompensated care," is passed on as higher costs to insured consumers. This increases the individual premiums of paying customers.

In 2008, that private "hidden tax" was about $1,017 in additional premiums per family.[8]

Businesses should support affordable, transferable insurance for all Americans as well. Insured workers are healthier and more productive, which makes our economy more competitive. About $200 billion is lost each year due to uninsurance.[9] Workers who can take their insurance with them when they change jobs make for a mobile workforce, and flexibility equals efficiency in the marketplace. Providing insurance to everyone spreads the risk and reduces overall costs for everyone. Universal access means better preventative care and increased early detection and treatment of serious medical problems. You can choose to pay a little for those tune-ups, or a lot more when your head gasket blows because you didn't change the oil.

The truly critical issues were not addressed adequately, if at all, in the 2009 health care debate. Why do we spend more than double the amount on our care compared to other developed countries, particularly when our results are often not as good? Why do Americans need so much more care than other people? Are we spending on the things that really work? Why does health care cost so much? Let's get pragmatic and dissect these issues before we worry about who pays the outrageous bills.

As a nation, we pride ourselves on being a tough, independent people. Our role models are the same in every generation—rugged, smart renegades like John Wayne or Matt Damon. But the truth is not so flattering. The Centers for Disease Control have a name for us—"obesogenic"—a society characterized by an environment that promotes increased food intake, non-healthful foods, and physical inactivity.

A perfect storm is brewing. We lead sedentary lives, eat garbage, absorb countless untested chemicals through food and other common products, rarely see primary care physicians before problems become critical and expensive, use drugs to address symptoms without tackling the underlying condition, rely on costly medical technology to "fix" us when we break—and to top it off, our kids are getting seriously ill at earlier ages, and we're all living longer. About 85 percent of our medical expenses are paid by insurers or the government (that's us—the taxpayers), so there is little impetus for individuals to do the healthy things that will save money.

Conventional Western medicine is geared toward treating disease, not keeping us healthy. In ancient China, it was just the opposite. The physician was paid to keep you well; if you got sick, the doctor had failed. He had to advertise that fact to other patients by hanging a certain lantern outside the office door. In America, 95 percent of the $2.5 trillion spent annually on health care is geared to treating disease *after* it occurs (and almost 70 percent of that money is spent on *10 percent* of the patients). Doctors do what they are trained and reimbursed to do—prescribe pills and perform surgeries—despite the real successes of preventive medicine and primary care that focus on keeping us healthy.

All told, almost a quarter of the nation's total health care expenditures, $493 billion, is attributed to smoking, obesity, and alcohol abuse.[10] I know that a small percentage of obese individuals and a few with alcohol dependence have a legitimate genetic problem. For everyone else, it is a matter of choice, of personal responsibility.

Our American lifestyle is responsible for most of the diseases we suffer. The treatment of diabetes, heart disease, breast and prostate cancer, and obesity absorb 75 to 80 percent of all medical costs, but often they are preventable and even reversible. As with alcohol or tobacco, stress is a leading contributor to many illnesses. Medication can provide relief, but it does nothing to halt the harmful, inflammatory adrenaline and cortisol that stress produces in our bodies. Changing our behavior along with our diet could do more to reduce health care costs than all the high-tech treatments and magical medicines put together. For most people, this is an issue of education, diet, exercise, and regular checkups—medical maintenance.

If there's any doubt about the effects of our lifestyle, just look at American kids. In barely a generation, the obesity rate in children has more than tripled. Childhood obesity is as damaging to a youngster's health as smoking. Type Two diabetes is disabling our teenagers, and increasingly, young men succumb to coronary problems. These young people have medical problems that shouldn't crop up until at least middle age. There is a current and future price tag associated with this—and the *only cure* is preventive care.

Michelle Obama has taken on the issue of child nutrition and is working to educate the public about the dangers of poor nutrition. She is promoting healthy solutions to this crisis—fewer Big Macs and more fruits and vegetables, getting sugary soft drinks out of schools, and putting kids back on the playground. On November 23, 2010, Sarah Palin told Laura Ingraham's radio listeners that the First Lady "is on this [antiobesity] kick, right. What she is telling us is she cannot trust parents to make decisions for their own children, for their own families in what we should eat. [J]ust leave us alone, get off our back, and allow us as individuals to exercise our own God-given rights to make our own decisions and then our country gets back on the right track." Partisanship has become so extreme that promoting healthy eating is now portrayed as part of a socialist government plot.

Unhealthy eating is not just a matter of free choice, it is also a matter of cost, availability, and individual decisions influenced by relentless marketing. The overconsumption of fat, salt, and sugar is *killing* us, particularly our kids. Thanks to huge government subsidies, foods containing large amounts of these substances are cheap, filling, and unhealthy. No one is trying to regulate your personal salt shaker or the number of sugars you choose to add to your coffee, but the quantities that people consume *inadvertently* are staggering. As a result, health care costs are going through the roof. Those most affected are lower-income families who either do not realize the detrimental effects or cannot afford fresh, healthier alternatives.

If our government tries to balance the equation, all hell breaks loose. Just try to cut farm subsidies, or better yet, to tax some of those empty calories to discourage consumption or pay down the medical costs. During the health care debate, there was talk about increasing taxes on sugary drinks. The beverage lobby unleashed a huge ad campaign. They attacked the liberal "nanny state" for trying to manipulate our behavior and regulate our choices. This same argument is used to oppose regulation of sodium and high-fructose corn syrup (HFCS) in packaged foods. The marketing campaign for HFCS is extraordinary. "Average" moms look into the camera and tell us that the syrup has the same calories as cane sugar, that our bodies don't know the difference. What they don't tell you is that HFCS is almost unavoidable in virtually all processed foods, especially those marketed to children. People have no idea that they are consuming this stuff in alarming quantities.

If the government regulates or taxes foods solely because some bureaucrat doesn't think you should eat burgers or drink soda pop—that's objectionable. But if substances in prepared foods are sickening the entire population and dramatically increasing health care costs for everyone, that is a problem we need to address. The move to eliminate trans fats from our foods is an excellent example. This artificial substance, cheap and convenient, was used primarily to increase a product's shelf life and reduce the need for refrigeration. A 2006 study in the *New England Journal of Medicine* concluded that up to one hundred thousand cardiac deaths each year were attributable to consumption of trans fats.[11] Research also links this substance to many other health risks, including serious liver problems, Alzheimer's, and even infertility in women. Cities and states took the lead in seeking voluntary cooperation from manufacturers. When corporations made it clear they weren't going to budge, only then did legislators step in. Today, many companies tout the absence of trans fats on the front of their packaging. It is amazing what a little consumer knowledge and pressure can do. Citizens in the 1800s understood this. Why don't we?

Substances like trans fats and HFCS must be dealt with through regulation because they cannot be separated from the end product. Such items as alcohol and tobacco, even soft drinks, are a different story. These are the items subject to so-called "sin taxes." Such taxes have been around since George Washington's administration slapped one on alcohol. Taxes have been a very effective way to reduce smoking, a behavior that imposes enormous costs on taxpayers. In New York City, exorbitant cigarette taxes coupled with a free nicotine patch program have reduced the number of smokers from 21.5 to 15.6 percent in the last eight years. Mayor Bloomberg is hoping to bring this down another 29 percent during his third term. This is about individual decisions that end up costing the community in taxpayer dollars, lost productivity, and countless other ways, both measurable and intangible. You are free to smoke or drink, but it should affect only *you*.

Maybe the most disturbing argument against a potential tax on sugary drinks or regulation of sodium is set out in the 1999 "Death-Savings" Report that tobacco giant Philip Morris wrote for officials in the Czech Republic (and publicly apologized for in 2001). It argued, quite convincingly, that the financial benefits for the nation from smoking outweighed the liabilities. The benefits in the report were listed as follows: increased revenue from taxes collected from the import and sale of cigarettes, taxes from corporate revenues, savings in health care, pension, and social expenses due to early mortality, and savings on housing for the elderly because they're dead. Unfortunately, to get those "cost savings," there were up-front expenses: direct and related health care costs, lost income from missed workdays, lost taxes from higher mortality, and for smokers. Even fire-induced costs made the list. But killing 'em off means more revenue up front and fewer costs later on. So let's forget instituting higher taxes that might reduce destructive behavior and its consequences. Instead, we can rejoice at the lower number of kids that will reach old age and all the long-term savings we'll experience.

Come on, nation. Get a grip. No one wants a nanny state, but we keep sticking our own fingers in the light socket. If we were just electrocuting ourselves, hey, go for it, but we're shorting out the entire house. Those obese kids will overtax the health care system and run up everyone's costs. They won't be healthy, productive taxpayers, so everything from Social Security to unemployment and welfare rolls will be affected. And not to go soft here, but they will face physical, social, and psychological hurdles they shouldn't have to encounter. Life is hard enough without that baggage.

Today, overweight people scream about liberty and personal rights and allege discrimination if they're told to buy two airline seats or pay a premium for their insurance, but they don't mind sticking us with the tab for their bad decisions. As with the banks that are too big to fail, we've developed a social moral hazard by having the insurance companies and government pick up most of our health care costs. Ultraconservative Arizona governor Jan Brewer is bucking Sarah Palin and other health care deniers and pushing for an annual tax on Medicare patients who are overweight, smoke, or refuse to follow doctor's orders in managing their chronic diseases. The choice is inevitable—either people bear the cost of their personal decisions or the taxpayer must do so. Then again, we can continue to defund public hospitals and emergency rooms and raise insurance rates, and simply step over bodies when they fall in the streets. That is an option.

There is a well-respected philosophical argument for promoting healthy decisions by enacting regulations and sin taxes. John Stuart Mill writes in *On Liberty*, "The only purpose for which power can be executed over any member of a civilized community against his will is to prevent harm to others." But Mill goes on to develop the "harm principle." Since we do not live in isolation, certain things that seem to affect only the actor actually hurt others. Mill includes the nonpayment of taxes as something that harms others. So, while we shouldn't take away the freedom to smoke or overeat, it is fair to incentivize healthy conduct or even enact taxes to cover the costs the rest of us bear when someone exercises freedom of choice and ends up on a ventilator or dialysis machine.

While the 2009 health care bill does include money for more preventive care, it poses a problem of the good old capitalist sort. Preventive care is cheap, so the doctors and hospitals make less money treating you up front. Writing out an exercise and diet plan, then monitoring your progress, doesn't rack up the revenue. A new marketing trick—a big moneymaker—is now part of the prevention game. Rather than regular checkups, early detection, and changing our lifestyles, big drug makers are now telling us that prevention should include the taking of various drugs if we have *any* risk factors that might potentially produce disease. That's a lot easier than refusing dessert or doing some cardio.

This spring, the FDA approved Crestor, a prescription cholesterol medication, for people *with no cholesterol problems*. If you're *healthy* but over fifty (men) or sixty (women) and have one risk factor, such as high blood pressure, you're a candidate for this statin drug. *Ninety-seven percent* of the U.S. population in that age group qualifies. The study that prompted FDA approval was funded, of course, by the drug's maker, which has already annual sales of $4.5 billion on Crestor along with a patent monopoly until 2016. The increased use of this drug among healthy people would add about $10 billion in health care costs. Researchers esti-

mate that saving one life in this expanded group would cost about
$557,000.[12] Statins help reduce inflammation; diet and stress are
the major causes. Instead of eating fruits and veggies, or exercising
for half an hour three days a week, we're encouraged to just pop a
pill, thereby putting billions in the pockets of the drug company.
This money-making gimmick pushes "preventive" drugs, which always have side effects, rather than encouraging healthy and relatively *cheap* lifestyle changes that *eliminate* high cholesterol and
high blood pressure. Maybe you should take some Prozac before
reading further—you might get depressed!

Then again, maybe not. Antipsychotic drugs, also prescribed for
depression, anxiety, and mood swings, are bestsellers, generating
$22 billion in global sales in 2008. When did we all get so crazy?
Numerous studies of this class of medication show that placebos
are as effective. Recent reports not only challenge whether they
work but also raise disturbing questions about their contribution
to premature death. In a 2008 report in the *Public Library of Science* journal, researchers said that for all but the most severely depressed, Prozac (and other related drugs) has little if any effect.[13]
The drug companies know that psychiatrists and patients ignore
these findings.

It is a good thing that society is more accepting of psychiatric
disorders. There is little stigma attached to a diagnosis of depression or anxiety. I am not advocating we reverse this important
trend. However, the pharmaceutical marketing departments figured out how to play this development to their advantage, and
sadly, plenty of doctors are cooperating. Now, a single symptom has
become a full-blown clinical disorder. Every mood fluctuation or
personality quirk is a syndrome, complete with an assortment of
drugs for treatment. Just watch the TV commercials if you need
verification. This gimmick has increased Big Pharma's customer
base by millions of individuals, and its sales revenues have soared.

Not surprisingly, abuse of prescription medications is a much bigger problem than the abuse of illegal drugs.[14] I don't know about you, but this makes me sick.

The United States and New Zealand are the only countries that allow direct-to-consumer marketing of prescription drugs. Before 1998, the Food and Drug Administration (FDA) prevented pharmaceutical companies from pitching prescription drugs directly to the public, fearing the very results that have come to pass. Drugs are now just another commodity. False and misleading ads are everywhere, "new" diseases crop up regularly, and overmedication is a huge problem. According to the Kaiser Family Foundation, every dollar spent marketing drugs to consumers produces an additional four dollars in sales. That's billions of dollars annually. FDA studies show people now expect there's a prescription for every problem. They go to their doctors asking for those purple pills by name, and the physicians usually comply.

Early in the health care negotiations, the drug industry considered relinquishing the ability to deduct advertising costs as a tradeoff for other favors. The media and marketing lobbyists went crazy. "Advertising deductibility safe!" was the headline in American Advertising Federation executive Clark Rector's press release when this idea was tabled. He noted that ending such tax breaks "would be a disastrous choice, both economically and politically" for these mad men—oops, I mean ad men. Our spending on prescription drugs is the fastest-growing health care cost. Heaven forbid we should put on the brakes.

And don't forget the scariest caveat of all, a little nugget for those who refuse to believe in evolution. While we've been gobbling all those antibiotics and feeding them to our livestock, those darn microbes have been reproducing offspring that laugh at our efforts. Overuse of antibiotics encourages the targets of these drugs to evolve, and sure enough, many are now immune to our medicines.

One "superbug," MRSA, now kills more people in the United States than HIV and AIDS, about nineteen thousand annually.[15] And a new wave of "super superbugs" (that's not a misprint) is sweeping the planet. But only two big drug companies are still doing major work in antibiotic research and development. It is more lucrative to produce weight loss products. Our FDA commissioner is screaming about this, and no one seems to be listening. Providing government research and adding in the typical tax breaks, subsidies, and patent protections would provide the needed impetus to tackle this problem. This is exactly the sort of thing incentives should be used for.

What are the other big costs in our health care system that must be addressed? Let's turn to the doctors and hospitals. A recent study by PricewaterhouseCoopers' Health Research Institute identified six primary areas where we *waste* about one-quarter of the $2.2 trillion spent annually on health care: unnecessary testing, $210 billion; insurance paperwork, $210 billion; using the costly ER as a routine clinic, $14 billion; medical errors, $17 billion; early patient discharge, $25 billion; and very preventable hospital infections, $3 billion.[16]

This massive waste is made possible because of the way our health care system is set up. We pay by the service rather than the outcome, so doctors are encouraged to overtest and overtreat. Hospitals discharge patients too early so they can readmit them with a whole new list of charges when they return with complications. With no coordinated record-keeping, tests are duplicated, doctors don't communicate, and medical errors increase. The opportunity for additional waste and fraud is magnified by the fragmented processing of claims.

Many doctors practice what is known as "defensive medicine," ordering unnecessary tests and medications and driving up the cost of medical care. Usually, conservatives blame malpractice costs for this overtreatment. I'm all for legitimate tort reform, as I detailed in my book *The Case Against Lawyers*, but it's a relative nonstarter for real health care savings. About 2 to 3 percent of medical negligence cases lead to a malpractice claim, and the Congressional Budget Office estimates that implementing standard tort reform proposals nationwide would cut our total U.S. health care spending by about 0.5 percent (about $11 billion in 2009). Harvard economist Amitabh Chandra counsels both the American Medical Association and trial lawyers on this issue and has calculated that the actual direct health care costs of lawsuits, including jury awards and settlements, are minuscule—less than 1 percent of such costs, while the total cost of defensive medicine is about 3 percent of all health care costs. Chandra's conclusions? We spend $150 billion a year because providers overtreat patients *to make more money*, not to avoid lawsuits.

Texas enacted tort reform several years ago, virtually eliminating malpractice suits, but in 2009, the state made headlines when a case study of the town of McAllen was released. Enterprising reporters wanted to know why, with the nation's lowest average household income, it had the country's second-highest per capita health care expenditures. It wasn't because of the trial lawyers—the lawsuits had disappeared. Its citizens were not sicker than those in neighboring counties. McAllen's care was no better; in fact it was often worse than care in other towns. Annually, Medicare was spending three thousand dollars more per person in this town than the average resident made in income all year!

A McAllen general surgeon told the reporter, "There is overutilization pure and simple. The way to practice medicine has changed completely. Before, it was about how to do a good job. Now it's about 'How much will you [the health care provider] benefit?'"[17] He explained that doctors and hospitals were ordering more procedures and services because they were paid more to do that.

The Dartmouth Institute produced a mammoth report in 2008 that concluded, unequivocally, that the more doctors, machines, testing, and hospital beds that were available in an area, the more we spent on health care—*with no improvement in outcomes*. The study looked at some of the most prestigious hospitals and clinics. UCLA Medical Center was "doing everything possible" for its patients while the Mayo Clinic and Cleveland Clinic were doing what the patients *really* needed. The institute concluded that the medical culture at UCLA encouraged the overuse of specialists and high-tech machinery—and the outcomes were no better, in fact, they were frequently worse than at the Mayo or Cleveland clinics. Think about it. The more medicines, the more surgeries and hospital stays, the more chances there are of complications, infections, and other negative results. Even without those dangers, the fact remains that all those specialists and fancy equipment were not helping and often were hurting patients. More is not always better, but it is more expensive.

We are learning about questionable or even dangerous surgeries that are commonly prescribed. In coronary care treatments, stents, bypasses, and other interventions do not repair the heart nor do they prevent future heart attacks (but they do cost $100 billion per year). Yet peer-reviewed studies show that heart disease can be both prevented and reversed through diet and exercise. Why isn't this approach the standard of care in American hospitals? Money. The same is true for many orthopedic interventions that tackle common joint and low back problems. In September 2008, the *New England Journal of Medicine* reported that arthroscopic knee surgery for arthritis is *ineffective*. The operation runs about five thousand dollars and is performed on hundreds of thousands of patients a year. This study reaches the same conclusions as one in 2002 that concluded the operations were "no better than a sham procedure."

Over a half million women have hysterectomies every year. It is the most commonly performed nonobstetric surgery in the United States, costing about $17 billion per year, and yet the experts tell us that a vast majority of these surgeries are unnecessary. Nearly one-third of the 4.3 million births in the United States are by Caesarean section, which has a four-times-higher risk of complications than natural delivery. It costs about twice as much but is very convenient. All told, U.S. doctors perform more than 60 million surgeries every year. How many of these are unnecessary? A lot.

If many conventional treatments had to meet medical evidentiary hurdles, they would not pass the tests. Federal funding for comparative effectiveness research was appropriated this year by Democrats to examine the problem, provoking objections that some bureaucrat will use the results to limit health care. This rational approach was first suggested by Republicans in the early nineties, but now, you guessed it, they oppose such research. Nothing could be more conservative in principle, or more philosophically Republican. Instead of throwing our money away, we should ask—what is the cost versus the true benefit? Whether it is an EPA proposal or a surgical technique, such pragmatic business analysis has always been a Republican talking point, yet because the Democrats adopted the idea, the GOP now opposes it. Appeasing its corporate contributors is more important than intellectual integrity.

Doctors are trained to save lives, and yes, that's what they're paid to do, but it is fair to examine what this means. Considering the cost and benefit of a treatment is particularly important when treating chronic disease or end-of-life cases. In a *60 Minutes* piece on end-of-life care, eighty-five-year-old Dorothy Gals, a former nurse, was profiled. She suffered from advanced heart and liver disease. "She had a living will stating that no extraordinary measures should be taken. Yet in that time period, she was seen by twenty-five specialists, each of whom billed Medicare separately. . . . A pap smear for an eighty-five-year-old woman dying of liver and heart disease is not typical, but that test was performed. She even had to see a psychiatrist, because her treating physicians said she was depressed. She told the psychiatrist, 'Of course I'm depressed. I'm dying.'" The hospital said the tests were appropriate, and the program's independent consultant said "this case was fairly typical."

As the baby boomers age and our life spans increase, we should be talking about end-of-life issues thoughtfully and rationally. Amazingly, a provision to allow Medicare to reimburse people for voluntary consultations became a plot to kill Grandma. This idea was suggested first in a bipartisan bill cosponsored by several Republicans, including Congressman and heart surgeon Charles Boustany. He says the conversations are good medical practice and should be encouraged and reimbursed. After starting the rumor that such counseling would be mandatory and was intended to limit end-of-life care, former New York lieutenant governor Betsy McCaughey finally backed off her claim, but the political damage was done. Many people still believe this is true.

A 2010 study in the *New England Journal of Medicine* reported that "42 percent of Americans over the age of 60 end up having to make some kind of decision about their medical care and, of those, 70 percent are incapable of doing so."[18] End-of-life discussions are known as "the multimillion-dollar conversation" because most terminal patients and their families then choose home or hospice care over expensive, intrusive hospital stays. This deprives the doctors and hospitals of serious income, so don't imagine that the health care providers are pushing for hospice over intensive care.

Medical technology is a blessing and a curse. We have amazing abilities to keep someone alive, but the quality of that life is one issue and another is the cost. A disproportionate amount of our health care dollars is spent on critical care at the end of life—about 10 to 12 percent of the total health care budget and 27 percent of the Medicare budget.[19] But in the Dartmouth Institute study referred to above, researchers found that more specialists, treatment, and hospital admissions didn't buy people more time. "In fact, patients with the more intensive and expensive treatment tended to die slightly sooner."

The entire medical-insurance complex has to change. We have to change. Our health care system must focus on wellness and prevention; it's simply a good business model for the nation. We should understand which treatments, pills, and surgeries work and which ones do not. Our medical care shouldn't be a marketing game. We should be told about end-of-life options and make informed decisions about the way we choose to spend our last days. Americans should quit subsidizing damaging products and, instead, voluntarily tackle the lifestyle issues that are costing us a fortune and are making us sick as a nation. You can have it all if you can afford it— but don't expect the rest of us to pay for it.

And pay for it we do. That nice health insurance policy you get through your employer is heavily subsidized by the government. Why? Because for the company, the insurance is a 100 percent tax writeoff, and the benefit to the employee is not taxed as income. This tax exclusion will cost the government more than one billion dollars over the next five years. Only self-employed individuals get the same treatment. Because of this, businesses can offer better plans. They don't have a big reason to pressure insurance companies to reduce expenses, and unless you have a high deductible, you don't either.

But there's a catch. Premiums are growing so fast that smaller companies are having trouble with the up-front expenses despite deductibility. Big corporations can bear the load. If this cost drives the little guys out of the market—tough luck and good riddance. Of course, many low-wage workers aren't offered insurance through their work or can't afford the copayments they'd have to make. But they have almost no power in Washington, so we ignore them.

It was a fluke of history that we got employers involved in medical coverage in the first place. Early insurance plans were benevolent gestures by a few employers, but in the 1940s, wage and price controls prevented salary increases. Offering health benefits became a tool to woo and keep workers. The concept took off, and we've had it ever since. In the past, this made some sense. Many people were lifelong employees of a single company. There was a cradle-to-grave idea of paternalistic protection for the "family," and often, health problems were work related. But today, this makes little sense. We're told to stay flexible, keep learning, and be prepared to change jobs at least five times in our careers. Health care should be attached to and move with the individual employee.

Economists tell us that one of the main reasons that wages have been flat for three decades is that employers have been putting your raise into their health care costs, including paying a human resources staff to manage your plan. Wouldn't you rather have more money and the ability to go purchase the coverage you want? The health insurance and tax deduction would be yours if you change jobs, leave the workforce, or become self-employed. If everyone bought his or her own plan, the insurance companies would treat us as their *real* customers, and we might pay attention to what we're spending and how to stay well.

The time has come for basic universal coverage. This can be public or private, but everyone should be insured—individually. Economics professor Peter Diamond at MIT has a simple, elegant solution for universal insurance coverage. Let the government create insurance pools based on where people live, ranging in size from ten thousand to one hundred thousand participants. A little gerrymandering of districts can make sure the poorer, less healthy people are pooled with more affluent neighborhoods to spread the risk. Then, private companies can bid on the contract to provide *basic* insurance to the members of each group. Of course, people could buy all the additional private insurance they desire, but this would provide the essential coverage people need so desperately while keeping the health care business in private hands.

I understand the whole liberty argument against mandatory coverage: The government should not force us to buy insurance. This position made sense when a trip to the doctor cost a few bucks, and an X-ray was the fanciest machine in the hospital. If someone failed to pay the bill, the doctor or hospital could absorb the cost. But circumstances have changed. Today, uninsured or underinsured people are sticking the rest of us with an enormous tab.

For those who argue that such a government mandate is unprecedented, check out the Militia Act of 1792. This was the first mandate I could find. Every able-bodied man was required to provide himself a long list of equipment, including "a good musket or firelock, a sufficient bayonet and belt, two spare flints, and a knapsack, a pouch." If you drive a vehicle, you have to purchase insurance. If you ever need medical care, well, you get the point. It's a no-brainer, just as the Republicans argued in 1993, and it's a windfall for the insurance industry.

We must corral our costs through legislation, regulatory reforms, personal responsibility, and a traditionally conservative cost-benefit/outcome-oriented health care system designed to promote wellness, not simply treat disease. Otherwise, we can simply follow the lead of other major industries and outsource our care. Health care tourism is a burgeoning new field. By 2011, about 6 million Americans will go to other countries for surgery. Some U.S. insurance plans now cover this expense. Fly to India to get that heart bypass surgery and it will cost you about $2,000 instead of the $20,000 to $100,000 here. Scary? Nope. Jack Lewin, the chief executive of the American College of Cardiology, visited one very successful Bangalore hospital run by Mother Teresa's cardiac surgeon, Dr. Devi Shetty. Lewin was quite impressed and noted that the volume of operations performed in that facility improved the doctors' techniques. This hospital has better mortality rates than our own, according to the Society of Thoracic Surgeons.[20] Is Dr. Shetty working on the cheap? No, he made about five hundred thousand dollars last year. He is building a two-thousand-bed general hospital in the Cayman Islands right now, just an hour by plane from Miami, where procedures will be priced at least 50 percent lower than in the United States. Get your tickets now.

Health care is a huge problem, one that affects every aspect of our lives. We must understand just how much corporate America controls the entire spectrum, including government decision-making. When *everything* is driven by the almighty dollar—the medicines we take, the surgeries we have, the foods we consume—something's got to give. Right now it is the physical welfare of our citizens and the fiscal health of our country.

In its preamble, the Founders stated explicitly that our Constitution was established to promote the general welfare. Our economic, social, and national security requires a healthy human infrastructure, one that is accessible and affordable for all Americans. So let's get off our backsides, take a deep breath, and start marching for meaningful reform as if our lives depended on it, because they do.

# X.

## *Keeping America Safe*

[America has] abstained from interference in the concerns of others, even when conflict has been for principles to which she clings. . . . She well knows that by once enlisting under other banners than her own, were they even the banners of foreign independence, she would involve herself beyond the power of extrication, in all the wars of interest and intrigue, of individual avarice, envy, and ambition, which assume the colors and usurp the standard of freedom. The fundamental maxims of her policy would insensibly change from liberty to force. . . . She might become the dictatress of the world.

—*John Adams*

The means of defense against foreign danger historically have become the instruments of tyranny at home.

—*James Madison*

Since the close of World War II, our approach to national security has undergone dramatic changes. The U.S. military is a permanent presence around the world. It requires a large central government, a huge defense industry, and countless support services to manage and maintain operations.

American taxpayers bear much of the cost of policing the planet. We spend more on defense than at least the next fourteen nations combined; that alone should raise serious questions. For the first time since 1840, we are using deficit spending, not taxes, to fund major wars. Because other nations can count on our military establishment, they are able to use their money, resources, and human energies in more productive ways.

Today, we have chosen to fight the war on terror with traditional military tactics, using the mass and might of our defense establishment rather than the smaller intelligence network and covert strategies that are historically more effective in combating insurgent warriors. This broad mission has led the United States from Iraq and Afghanistan to Yemen, Sudan, Pakistan and beyond in just one decade.

The populist uprising in Tunisia sparked a wave of civil revolts across the Middle East. We are participating in a U.N.-backed military action in Libya. Long-standing regimes throughout the region are experiencing instability. The moment is ripe for a critical discussion of U.S. military policies and national security interests.

Diplomacy is a critical arm of our national security, yet there are more people in our military marching bands than in the State Department's Foreign Service.[1] The cost of maintaining a single soldier in Afghanistan for one year, between $500,000 and $1 million, could build a lot of infrastructure and goodwill, which is far more likely to win converts from the Taliban to our stated mission of stability and democracy.

Our national security policies affect every aspect of our society—culturally, politically, and economically. Americans will always rally to defend this great nation, but a true patriot never fears a serious debate about the methods we use to accomplish this vital mission.

How did our Founders address national security issues? Why

did the United States approach to international engagement change so dramatically about sixty years ago? What are the biggest threats to our homeland, our strategic interests, and the financial and physical well-being of the American people? What does the ostensibly democratic uprising in the Middle East mean for U.S. foreign policy? How can we, when they are needed, deploy our defense resources more safely, economically, and efficiently? Let's take a look.

Every generation faces threats that seem to imperil our very survival. Wars, financial crises, and social unrest test our commitment to democracy. For now, the Republic survives, but current national security and defense policies bear no relationship to our founding principles. The world has changed, but the underlying philosophy on which this nation was established is still valid.

Whether we should provide for the common defense is a no-brainer. The devil, of course, is in the details—defining the threats, determining the appropriate actions, and considering how far to extend our reach. Americans of all persuasions are intensely loyal to their country, but the statement, "You're either with us or against us," should be a red flag to any loyal citizen. It is a means of stifling debate and coercing agreement, a dangerous tactic when the nation contemplates military action.

I am a patriot, through and through. I believe in a strong military to defend American security at home and abroad. But what does this mean? In the twenty-first century, defining "security" is a daunting task. The variety of threats we face is increasing as are the methods required to repel them. The Founders feared armies and navies from Europe. Today, we do not worry about such traditional invasions. The Cold War gave rise to the threat of nuclear annihilation, but now, missiles fired by the governments of Russia or China are not our primary concern.

Today, we focus primarily on rogue states and independent terror organizations. These enemies cannot match our military might or our financial resources, but they don't need to. By drawing us into conflicts overseas, they drain those assets, shed American blood, and disrupt our domestic policies. Civilians in their countries pay a very high price, but often, those sacrifices are useful as propaganda and recruiting tools. Then there's the threat of another 9/11—a devastating attack within our porous borders. Terror groups know we will spend enormous sums, even violate American liberties, to thwart real or perceived dangers to the nation.

There are many new issues that affect our national security. In a world of diminishing resources, access to critical materials can be essential to stability, even survival. China controls much of the world's rare minerals, which are needed for essential new technologies, and they may not be inclined to share. People may argue about climate change, but whether part of some long natural cycle or essentially man-made, the problem is real. If you think oil is important, just wait until food and water scarcity dominates our headlines. Our military leaders know that warming temperatures and wildly fluctuating weather patterns will produce major social disruption and the potential for great conflict. People in hard-hit regions will try to migrate to more hospitable climes. Those left behind will fight over reduced resources. The Pentagon has been brainstorming these scenarios for more than a decade.

Cyberwarfare and the militarization of space are not sci-fi concepts. They are very real strategies already in play. Why should an advanced nation like China pour money into military hardware to counter threats from the West when a computer attack on our financial industry or energy grid would bring the United States to a halt? This threat was made clear in June 2010, when Iran's nuclear program was attacked by the Stuxnet virus, reportedly setting back its development by many months. This computer malware disabled Iranian computer systems without alerting workers that anything was amiss for quite some time. According to a report by the IT security company Symantec, "The real world implications of Stuxnet are beyond any threat we have seen in the past. Stuxnet is the type of threat we hope never to see again." While many unconfirmed reports credit the United States for this attack, our leaders have neither claimed nor denied responsibility. Other nations, particularly China, are investing tremendous resources into perfecting technologies that would make similar disruptions possible.

Finally, there's the spread of populist uprisings in authoritarian governments throughout the Middle East and North Africa. Thanks to modern technology and social networking, people in the most isolated regions now share our dreams of freedom and self-governance and believe they, too, can bring about democratic change. America's long-standing alliances with friendly tyrants are being called into question, forcing the ultimate Hobbesian choice upon this nation—do we stand for our most valued ideals and principles or don't we? Answering this in the affirmative doesn't mean we jump into every revolt with guns blazing, but it will reframe sixty years of foreign policy and reshape our relationships with governments around the world.

Unfortunately, America's national security responses are dictated by twentieth-century attitudes and institutions. Our actions and policies are draining valuable, even priceless, resources and threatening constitutional principles and fundamental values. Our notion of victory in the global war on terror is an elusive, misguided concept leading to strategies that exacerbate and expand the very conflicts we're engaged in. It is our patriotic duty to question the rationale, methods, and long-term repercussions of these policies.

For those who believe such inquiry is disloyal, read your history. There have been truly just wars. But most conflicts have been sold to the American people under false pretenses or with intentions that range well beyond our founding principles governing foreign entanglements. Leaders, both Republican and Democrat, have manipulated emotions, edited facts, and ignored critical information to sell their missions. It is worth noting how often these decision-makers look back on their own deeds with regret, hoping that future generations learn from their mistakes. We rarely do.

In 1776, the Founders disagreed about the break from England, but once the decision was made, they united around the call for independence. Ben Franklin reminded them, "We must all hang together, or assuredly we shall all hang separately." No one can doubt their commitment to defend this nation. However, these good patriots did not agree on military strategies during the war or on national security issues once the government was established. Debate and disagreement was integral to this democracy, and fight they did.

During the debates of 1787, many delegates to the Constitutional Convention opposed the Federalists' push for a strong standing army. A compromise was reached that established a national army but restrained its growth by constitutionally mandating that it receive funding for only two years at a time. The nation would rely most heavily on state-based militias (later the National Guard) for troops. A small army, the militias, and a healthy navy characterized our national defense until the Civil War.

After the government was established, Hamilton and Jefferson continued the ideological debates about national security and foreign policy. Hamilton was a military man to the core. Under George Washington, he used troops to subdue American citizens. When Britain and France went to war in 1793, he saw an opportunity and hinted that if America were to oppose France, it might be a good time to capture New Orleans or "liberate" Mexico from Spain. European wars were fought over territory primarily for economic reasons, and he wanted to push Europe out of North America, but Hamilton would never condone wasting our nation's resources policing the planet or exporting democracy. He was too much of a bottom-line realist.

Jefferson recognized that strength was a deterrent to conflict, but his writings are filled with pleas for peace and neutrality. In his inaugural address, Jefferson expressed his foreign policy succinctly: "Peace, commerce, and honest friendship with all nations, entangling alliances with none." He opposed the extension of American practices and ideals through the instruments of war. "For us to attempt by war to reform all Europe, and bring them back to principles of morality and a respect for the equal rights of nations, would show us to be only maniacs of another character."[2] Jefferson would have thought it the height of absurdity to try such intervention in places like Iraq or Afghanistan. From a purely economic perspective, Jefferson, like Adam Smith, believed that war was a tremendous drain on economic and human resources. Only events that posed a direct threat to America should give rise to war, and then, only as a last resort.

By 1823, our young Republic was itching to expand its economic and political influence. The Monroe Doctrine, James Polk's Manifest Destiny, and Teddy Roosevelt's Corollary were presidential justifications for using the military to expand American territory and power. To this day some people still argue that we are divinely destined to spread democracy, but this was just a marketing ploy to justify a rather imperialistic mission to obtain more land, resources, and markets. The Europeans had done this for years, and for a time, our nation simply followed that playbook. It should be noted that conservatives took the lead in denouncing the policies and actions.

Despite this adventurism, we avoided foreign conflicts and our military remained small. Only when American lives were lost in German submarine attacks, and diplomacy failed to ensure the safety of our ships at sea, did we relent and enter World War I.

After the armistice in November 1918, our military was reduced to its prewar size and neutrality was again our foreign policy. In 1940, Americans were very divided about our possible involvement in World War II. The debate ended abruptly when Pearl Harbor was bombed, as did any meaningful isolationism in American foreign policy. When fighting ceased, our military remained to occupy Germany and Japan, and a turning point was reached. America was now a global economic, military, and political leader, and our reach has been expanding ever since.

Rather than reducing the military after World War II as we had in years past, we institutionalized this growing sector, and by the mid-1950s, we had embarked on a mission to contain communism halfway around the world. Our new attitudes about national security and foreign policy were no longer tied to America's founding principles nor to any military philosophy expressed by our early leaders, whether liberal or conservative.

Believing that the North Koreans and North Vietnamese were simply puppets of the Soviets and Chinese, we failed to understand the nature of the Korean and Vietnam wars, particularly how we would be perceived by the very populations we wanted to defend. Our nation was founded by guerilla fighters battling a foreign oppressor, yet we knew little about insurgency warfare. We still haven't learned those lessons.

In his inaugural address, President Kennedy pledged to "pay any price, bear any burden, meet any hardship, support any friend, oppose any foe, in order to assure the survival and success of liberty." He affirmed the policy of containment and believed that a limited conflict was possible in Vietnam. Yet shortly before his assassination, he called for a drawdown of U.S. military personnel. The South Vietnamese population perceived that Americans were propping up their corrupt government; we were part of the problem, not the solution. Without widespread support among the Vietnamese people, Kennedy realized, the United States could not win any long-term victory. But Kennedy's order to begin the pull-out was reversed when Lyndon Johnson took office.

A strong believer in the domino theory—that the fall of Vietnam would doom all of Southeast Asia—President Johnson had other ideas. He wanted an excuse to expand our military presence in the region, so he manufactured a good reason for members of Congress and the American people.

On August 2 and August 4, 1964, there were two allegedly unprovoked attacks on U.S. destroyers by North Vietnamese gunboats. President Johnson called for a resolution to support "all necessary action to protect our Armed Forces" while assuring that "the United States . . . seeks no wider war." News outlets gave the story dramatic, positive coverage, and Congress gave Johnson complete authority to respond in the Gulf of Tonkin Resolution passed on August 7. The president could now "take all necessary measures to repel any armed attack against the forces of the United States and to prevent further aggression." The war was on.

Classified information released in recent years tells a very different story. The United States was engaged in covert maritime raids on North Vietnamese coastal targets just before the Gulf of Tonkin events. On August 2, a U.S. destroyer on an electronic espionage mission fired on North Vietnamese gunboats. The U.S. destroyer suffered a single machine-gun round as damage. The second "attack" *never* occurred. Johnson's Department of Defense wanted an escalation, and these "events" created the justification they'd been looking for.

In 2005, the *New York Times* reported that the National Security Agency kept its 2001 discovery of these classified materials secret. Confirmation that the Gulf of Tonkin incidents were a ruse to expand our military involvement would have invited "unfavorable comparisons with the flawed intelligence used to justify the war in Iraq."[3]

We cannot prevent determined officials from deceiving the peo-

ple. After all, Secretary of State Colin Powell chose following orders over the truth when he delivered phony intelligence on Iraq
to the United Nations. But this is harder to pull off when our constitutional provisions and democratic philosophy are respected.
Transparency in government, a true balance of power between
Congress and the executive branch, substantive public debate, and
a fourth branch, the press, that takes its adversarial role seriously—
all were designed to prevent or limit such overreaching.

There are other critical lessons from Vietnam that we ignore at
our peril. Determined insurgents are almost impossible to defeat,
even with overwhelming force. According to the official history of
the U.S. Army, "In Vietnam, the Army experienced tactical success
and strategic failure." In a secret memo to President Ford, U.S. secretary of state Henry Kissinger wrote, "In terms of military tactics,
we cannot help draw the conclusion that our armed forces are not
suited to this kind of war. Even the Special Forces who had been
designed for it could not prevail."

The United States is not alone in such failure. Assessments by
Soviet generals of their war in Afghanistan are virtually identical.
That war cost the Soviets billions of rubles and countless lives and
ended in defeat. The Soviet-installed government was overthrown
within four years, lasting not much longer than the South Vietnamese government did after the United States withdrew.

Our venture in Afghanistan is just another textbook demonstra-
tion that a large foreign force is rarely capable of defeating a determined insurgency. This outcome does not change with the size
or quality of the foreign military. It is contingent on the internal
politics of the war-torn nation. An outside army cannot prop up
corrupt and oppressive leaders and antagonize a native population
with civilian casualties and then expect the broad cooperation necessary to isolate and defeat insurgents. What may be perceived as
success vanishes quickly when troops are withdrawn.

Guerilla forces are quite capable of going to ground and waiting for years if necessary. If the foreign military instigates a major push into a region, the insurgents just move out and wait or increase attacks in other areas. The larger, less nimble foreign force must either scatter its troops or remain locked down to hold an area it has cleared. The insurgents simply pick their battles—striking at will then blending back into the local population. Invariably, foreign troops will injure or kill many civilians when pursuing guerilla fighters. These casualties destroy local support and become an excellent recruiting tool for the guerillas. It is worth reading George Polk's history of insurgency, *Violent Politics*, to truly understand the nature of these conflicts.

The point is not to abandon our goal of defeating terrorism but to examine our strategies, particularly the rationale for all-out war. The U.S. policy of major intervention in response to regional disruptions or isolated terrorism is a relatively new development, one that bears no relationship to our traditional ideals.

The policies that led us into expanded wars in Iraq and Afghanistan were instigated by leaders of the neoconservative movement that emerged in the 1960s and reached its high point during George W. Bush's administration. True believers like Dick Cheney, Donald Rumsfeld, and Paul Wolfowitz were determined to expand American influence and their notion of "friendly democracies" through the use of military force. The neocons still believe that our way (*their* way) is the only way, and more important, that U.S. policies must be imposed throughout the world to protect American interests.

The neocons were not happy with the first George Bush. On February 13, 1992, a draft of a classified Pentagon report, now known as the "Wolfowitz Doctrine" was leaked to the *New York Times* in hopes of generating public debate over its radical proposals. Essentially, the new doctrine asserted that America would go it alone in the world. Our long-standing policy of internationalism, of working with allies, was rejected. We were the world's lone superpower, and we would act unilaterally when our economic or military order was disturbed, even when conflicts did not involve U.S. interests directly.[4] Neocon Ben Wattenberg explained, "America is No. 1. We stand for something decent and important. That's good for us and good for the world. That's the way we want to keep it."[5]

The document created an uproar. Here was a blanket declaration that America had the right to remake the world as it pleased. Bush 41 acted quickly to quash this proposal by issuing a new report that reaffirmed our long-standing belief in international cooperation.

With the president's policies back on track, Secretary of Defense Dick Cheney delivered an assessment of the first Iraq war in August 1992. Capturing Saddam wouldn't be worth additional U.S. casualties or the risk of getting "bogged down in the problems of trying to take over and govern Iraq. . . . All of a sudden you've got a battle you're fighting in a major built-up city, a lot of civilians are around, significant limitations on our ability to use our most effective technologies and techniques. . . . Once we had rounded him up and gotten rid of his government, then the question is what do you put in its place? You know, you then have accepted the responsibility for governing Iraq."[6] As intended, his comments appeased the critics, but Cheney's neocons experienced only a temporary setback. They would find means and opportunity to pursue their strategies under like-minded George W. Bush. The events of 9/11 gave the Bush administration carte blanche to implement them.

On 9/11, al Qaeda operatives attacked the World Trade Center and the Pentagon. In a televised address to a joint session of Congress on September 20, Bush launched the plan. "Our 'war on terror' begins with al Qaeda, but it does not end there. It will not end until every terrorist group of global reach has been found, stopped and defeated." At that moment, every American was filled with grief and anger. Bush's sentiments were understandable.

On September 14, 2001, the House of Representatives (420–1) and the Senate (98–0) authorized the president to "use all necessary and appropriate force against those nations, organizations, or persons he determines planned, authorized, committed, or aided the terrorist attacks that occurred on September 11, 2001, or harbored such organizations or persons." Yet most Americans believed our targets were Osama bin Laden and al Qaeda training camps. Publicly, U.S. leaders assured the Afghan people that they were not the enemy. Then things got very murky.

Few Americans realized Bush intended a full-scale military intervention in Afghanistan, or that he would soon justify a doctrine of preemptive war against other nations. Neocon Robert Kaplan described how this policy should be sold to the American people. "'Only through stealth and anxious foresight' can the United States continue to pursue the 'imperial reality [that] already dominates our foreign policy,' but [it] must be disavowed in light of 'our anti-imperial traditions.'" He acknowledged that the strategy is in conflict with America's founding principles—this is not what we stand for—but by appealing to national security, the Bush administration "has kept as many of those actions as it can secret and has scorned all limitations to executive power by other branches of government or international law."[7]

The neocons crafted a more targeted approach for their conservative Christian base, just as they're doing today. They pitched this strategy as a modern-day crusade against the entire Muslim world—a united enemy seeking to destroy not only America but Christianity itself. The "end times" were close at hand. While religious conservatives proclaim allegiance to founding principles, they lose the thread entirely when the Bible is thrust into the debate. And their favored politicians ring that bell as often and as loudly as they can.

Pat Buchanan described the neocon approach as a "a globalist, interventionist ideology."[8] Nationalism and fear are the psychological tools and major budget deficits are the financial ones used to accomplish far-ranging goals. By selling the American people on a doomsday scenario requiring preemptive action, the neocons were able to both ramp up military spending and shrink "liberal" social programs. We were facing huge deficits, but survival trumps everything else. If there is no money left for social programs after defense spending, well, at least we're still alive. Maybe there's no Social Security, health care, or national infrastructure, but hey, we're defeating distant infidels—you can't have everything. This strategy is being replayed in the 2011 deficit debate.

The neocons had set the mood and now began to execute their plan. The first step was an invasion of Iraq. Their objective of regime change throughout the Middle East was no secret. It was clearly spelled out in their Project for the New American Century publications. This invasion and how to divide Iraq's oil revenues had been discussed in President Bush's earliest cabinet meetings in January 2001—eight months before 9/11.[9] Saddam Hussein had been propped up by the United States for years, but of late, he'd wandered off the reservation. An avid secularist who opposed al Qaeda, he had incurred neocon wrath by bucking U.S. directives and threatening to destabilize other friendly regimes.

We know now that intelligence reports were manufactured to forge a link between Saddam Hussein and al Qaeda that would establish an imminent threat to the United States "in the form of a mushroom cloud." Based on such information, Congress authorized President Bush to use the military "as he determines to be necessary and appropriate" in order "to defend the national security of the United States against the continuing threat posed by Iraq." President Bush signed this blank check on October 16, 2002 and began preparing for the invasion.

The goal of overthrowing Saddam Hussein morphed quickly into the goal of establishing a functioning democracy in the heart of the Middle East. After a decade of fighting, we still cling to that same objective in historically lawless Afghanistan. Our Founders considered European conflicts to be disastrous quagmires. Just imagine how they'd react to our present-day conflicts. George Polk offers this insight:

> American forces have been sent abroad to fight more than two hundred times since our country was founded. But in recent years, only sixteen times have we attempted "the core objective of nation building [or] regime change." . . . Of these sixteen . . . eleven were "outright failures." Two, Germany and Japan, can be regarded as successes, while two others, tiny and nearby Grenada and Panama, were probably successful. Considering this record . . . how could neoconservatives or any conservatives "who normally don't trust their government to run a public school down the street, come to believe that federal bureaucrats could transform an entire nation in the alien culture of the Middle East?" [10]

General David Petraeus's 2006 counterinsurgency manual described the problems of insurgency warfare, but it offered no new solutions. Every single tactic Petraeus lists, from "winning the hearts and minds" to "hold and clear" have been tried by other great military powers, and they have failed, just as those strategies are failing us today. This is *not* a criticism of our troops or our military leadership. They are the best in the world. It is a criticism of their mission.

In his manual, General Petraeus recites truths that should give us pause. "[Killing insurgents] cannot defeat an insurgency . . . killing every insurgent is normally impossible [and] counterproductive in some cases; it risks generating popular resentment, creating martyrs that motivate new recruits, and producing cycles of revenge." He continues, "The more force applied, the greater the

chance of collateral damage and mistakes . . . [increasing] the opportunity for insurgent propaganda to portray lethal military activities as brutal." If you read the stories about drone attacks and
civilian deaths, you know that even carefully targeted assaults can
build opposition among the people we want to win over.

On its face, the goal is simply impossible. The enemy is like a
shape-shifter, here one minute and gone the next. Small cells or
individual terrorists, disconnected from any organized structure,
crop up all over the world. Most of them have no capability of acting outside their own territory, but they can wreak havoc against a
powerful military and their own civilian populations. This cycle of
violence is both organized and random. It can never be completely
eliminated, any more than every potential Timothy McVeigh can
be detected and deterred.

Despite his preelection opposition to the war in Iraq and promise to extricate us from Afghanistan, President Obama has continued the Bush policies with predictable results. Saddam Hussein
was a secular tyrant whose brutal regime suppressed religious and
ethnic tensions. When he was overthrown, those disputes took center stage and spread to other nations, including Yemen and Sudan.
A weakened Iraq emboldened its historic rival, Iran. Obama offi-
cially ended the military action in Iraq by replacing troops with expensive private contractors. Elections in that country demonstrate
that voting is not enough to establish a democracy. Its leaders have
no concept of shared power and are unwilling to support a real
constitutional government. The violence continues, and war with
Iran is a major concern.

Prospects in Afghanistan are even worse. In October 2009,
Obama's national security advisor, General James Jones, gave an interview on CNN and estimated that fewer than one hundred members of al Qaeda remained in the country, yet President Obama
ordered a troop surge. After all, the goal was now the overthrow of
the Taliban and the establishment of a functioning democracy.

Our man in Kabul, Hamid Karzai, is a carbon copy of other despotic rulers put in power by foreign forces throughout history. Show me just one who stayed in power by implementing real democracy after his outside benefactors withdrew. (He doesn't exist.) Instead, Karzai has been straddling the fence and is now negotiating with the Taliban to maintain control.

Actually, we are talking with them as well. No Afghan government that ignores the Taliban has a chance of surviving when we leave. This is *realpolitik*—when idealism and moral principles give way to cold hard truths. Yet the American people have been sold the notion that the Taliban are evil, oppressive supporters of terrorism that must be overthrown. We have spent billions in borrowed money and have sent our young men and women into battle at great sacrifice—only to arrive where we began; negotiating a deal with the Taliban.

Worse yet, we have allowed our mission to creep into *very* dangerous territory as we step up incursions into Pakistan. Pakistan has been a questionable U.S. ally for years. Its intelligence agency, the ISI, uses terrorists to fuel tensions in the disputed region of Kashmir. Americans are viewed by Pakistanis as inherently suspect and too closely aligned with India. Our growing presence within its borders, especially with civilian deaths from U.S. drone attacks, has incited public outrage—again, creating potential terrorists among people who have no love for al Qaeda.

The potential for international disaster posed by Pakistan is as great as if not greater than that posed by Iran. In the 1990s, the United States halted weapons sales to Pakistan because of its nuclear weapons program, but after 2001, President Bush began sales again, and by 2006, it was our number one arms client. Pakistan is increasingly unstable and yet refuses any help to secure its nuclear arsenal. In October 2009, Prime Minister Yousaf Raza Gillani told his parliament that Pakistan "would never allow a foreign power to have access to Pakistan's nuclear assets." As the *New York Times* reported, this was in response to U.S. efforts to get more cooperation in securing its nuclear weapons materials. In 2010, U.S. officials expressed growing concern about possible attacks in the United States by Pakistan-based groups. Yet the United States proceeded to give this country another $2 billion in military aid—weaponry that may well be used against us in the future. Then there's Osama bin Laden, who was comfortably ensconced in a wealthy Pakistani neighborhood occupied primarily by that nation's retired military officers. The U.S. Navy Seal team that killed bin Laden did so without Pakistani knowledge, as U.S. officials feared our plans might be thwarted by Pakistani officials. As anger toward the United States increases among the general population, Pakistan's leaders are making overtures to the Chinese and announced $30 billion in new trade deals with that nation in early 2011. We manufacture and sell weapons; China profits from everything else.

For several decades, our policy on arms exports has been driven as much by corporate interests as by national security. In October 1991, delegates representing the five U.N. Security Council permanent members adopted guidelines to restrain the sale of conventional arms that would be likely to "(a) prolong or aggravate an existing armed conflict; (b) increase tension in a region or contribute to regional instability; (c) introduce destabilizing military capabilities in a region." In 1992, before the agreement could be concluded, George H. W. Bush agreed to sell 150 F-16 fighters to Taiwan. He was trailing in the polls, and those planes were coming from his electorally rich home state of Texas. China was incensed and abandoned the talks. The discussions have never resumed.[11]

Our official arms export policy talks about "promoting regional stability, ensuring U.S. military superiority, and promoting peaceful conflict resolution and arms control, human rights and democratization." But in February 1995, President Clinton issued Presidential Decision Directive 34 that added a new factor: "enhanc[ing] the ability of the U.S. defense industrial base to meet U.S. defense requirements and maintain long term military superiority at lower costs." Translation: our arms policy should also help our weapons manufacturers.

In the past decade, "the majority of U.S. arms sales to the developing world went to countries that our own State Department defined as undemocratic regimes and/or major human rights abusers." Overall sales increased more than 50 percent from 2007 to 2008, and the numbers climbed again in 2009.[12] According to the New American Foundation, in 2009, "The volume of global defense contracts involving the United States exceeded those of all other countries combined." As we deliberate on the growing unrest throughout the Middle East, ship weapons to the latest freedom fighters, and send our military to help these rebels, remember—once again, we've armed both sides of the conflict and are ducking our own bullets. As with the mujahideen in Afghanistan, we know little about these populist uprisings. I am a tremendous supporter of the grassroots revolutions in the Middle East and believe they are legitimate movements, but as we indiscriminately arm these fighters, it is inevitable that terrorist groups will benefit as well.

Scaling back corporate and government weapons sales may be a bridge too far for this country, so what is the next-best strategy? On September 19, 2008, a RAND Corporation study, *Defeating Terrorist Groups*, was presented to the U.S. House Armed Services Committees. It recommended that the U.S. military "should generally resist being drawn into combat operations in Muslim countries where its presence is likely to increase terrorist recruitment." It concluded that "by far the most effective strategy against religious groups [Islamic fundamentalists] has been the use of local police and intelligence services, which were responsible for the end of 73 percent of [terrorist] groups since 1968."

This tactic was used successfully throughout the Cold War. It was not warfare that prevented nuclear annihilation. Instead, intelligence gathering, covert ops, and "carrot and stick" diplomacy were the critical tools. Yet Republicans have repeatedly criticized this "law and order" approach because their goals are not merely stopping terrorism; they want the expansion of American power, and, of course, both parties want to please the big defense contractors.

If we are truly the Republic envisioned by our Founders, we must rethink our use of military power. Our policies are threatening the economic well-being of our nation and corrupting the core American values we want the world to adopt. They require a permanent state of war, as our actions inspire more insurrection, not less. The purported goals—eliminating all terrorism and rapidly establishing democracies in countries that have no cultural understanding of a self-governing system or the political infrastructure to support one—are unachievable. Ultimately, they are making America less secure at home and abroad.

When President Obama pushed for talks with Iran, George H. W. Bush's secretary of state, Jim Baker, stated emphatically that "diplomacy is not appeasement." He was a strong opponent of Cheney's philosophy when they served together and has remained so to this day. The bigger and more powerful a nation is, the more it can and should talk. The fall-back position, military muscle, is always there. As Thomas Jefferson and Adam Smith warned, and history validates, the cost of using force can be much higher for the victor than for the vanquished.

Our leaders show little sign of changing course. The Department of Defense delivered its Quadrennial Defense Review to Congress in February 2010 describing its twenty-year projection for U.S. military planning. There are several major priorities. First, we must "prevail in today's wars," which include Afghanistan, Iraq, Pakistan, and Yemen. Defense Secretary Robert Gates said that "success in wars to come depends on success in these wars [now] in progress."

These conflicts are "only the first step toward achieving our strategic objectives." Second, we need "a robust force capable of protecting US interests against a multiplicity of threats, including two capable nation-state aggressors." Thus we must be able to handle two major wars plus counterinsurgency and counterterrorism operations and other disrupting events; all, it seems, without raising taxes or instituting a draft.[13]

Currently, there are about four hundred thousand U.S. military personnel deployed at one thousand overseas bases around the world. Our servicemen and women are second to none. For now, we are dominant in space. To maintain such supremacy, we currently spend more on defense than the next fourteen nations *combined*. China is second on the list followed by France, the United Kingdom, Russia, Germany, and Japan.[14] Why must we spend so much more—in money, resources, and lives—than these other global powers? Do they not take their own national security as seriously as we do?

And remember where the twenty-first-century threats are coming from. Our most feared enemy is the rogue terrorist with a suitcase nuke, but a new threat to national security, cyberterrorism, is looming large. In May 2010, the stock market plunged one thousand points in less than fifteen minutes. One of the first concerns was whether this was a cyberattack. An assault on our financial systems or energy grid could bring the nation to a halt and invoke mass panic around the world. Russians have been blamed for a major cyberattack on Estonia in 2007, and a series of coordinated hacks known as Titan Rain was carried out by Americans on various U.S. computer networks in 2003, including those at Lockheed Martin, Sandia National Laboratories, and NASA. Do we intend to marshal troops against every hacker on the planet? And don't forget the Stuxnet attack on Iran's nuclear weapons software. Our systems are vulnerable too.

And then there is WikiLeaks. The release of thousands of U.S. government communiqués on the Internet by its founder, Julian Assange, has exposed additional vulnerabilities intrinsic to this electronic age. Information can be as powerful a weapon as bullets or bombs. Assange has demonstrated that major institutions can be compromised in ways we never imagined, and he has inspired other groups to follow his lead. In June 2011, Sarah Palin mischaracterized events surrounding the midnight ride of Paul Revere. Presumably acting without direction from her, some Palin supporters tried to rewrite history on Revere's Wikipedia page to make it correspond with Sarah's rendition. Their changes were corrected immediately, but this minor incident shows us just how dangerous technology can be. What might occur if hackers could alter electronic government records, reports, and investigation materials? The implications are staggering.

The current economic crisis demonstrates how our national debt affects U.S. national security. What role does our weakened economy play in military decision making? Some will argue that this could mean dangerous cutbacks in our defense force, while others fear we may increase military activity to grow the economy. The late political columnist David Broder actually suggested attacking Iran would be a good political move for President Obama. "With strong Republican support in Congress for challenging Iran's ambition to become a nuclear power, he can spend much of 2011 and 2012 orchestrating a showdown with the mullahs. This will help him politically because the opposition party will be urging him on. And as tensions rise and we accelerate preparations for war, the economy will improve." [15]

Military decisions must not be justified by the need to boost our GDP, our tax revenues, or the profits of multinational corporations. But just try closing a military base or shutting down a major weapons system and see how quickly you are labeled as weak on defense. Time and again, the military brass tell Congress that certain weapons programs are unnecessary or simply unwanted, yet our legislators appropriate funds regardless. It's all about money (jobs are part of this economic issue), not our actual military needs or national defense. Major campaign finance reform, preferably through public financing, is the only remedy.

The incestuous relationship between our local, state, and national governments, defense industries, independent contractors, and our national debt is mind-blowing. This presents a tremendous threat to the Republic for myriad reasons that have nothing to do with national security. You can be a philosophical conservative, even a member of what some might term the far right, and still see the need to examine these issues and ask some probing questions. Simply waving the flag is not a legitimate or patriotic response.

One of the biggest conflicts for conservatives is the contradiction between supporting military spending and demanding small government. Americans must realize that we cannot have a far-reaching military presence around the world and a limited federal government at the same time. It is not possible. Let me restate this. If your idea of a strong national defense is represented by the military policies the nation has implemented since 2000, you *cannot* believe in a limited federal government, no matter how often you say that you do. Currently, our national defense involves millions of people spending trillions of dollars around the world. Huge corporations are entirely dependent on big military contracts for their existence. In recent years, we've seen an explosion of corruption, fraud, waste, and abuse that has accompanied the large-scale outsourcing of our military, defense, and homeland security functions. Continued privatization of our national defense is very dangerous for individual liberty, national security, and the Republic as a whole.

President Eisenhower would be horrified by the growth of the mercenary culture in our modern military. The day before the 9/11 terrorist attacks, "Secretary of Defense Donald Rumsfeld told his staff that the Pentagon was wasting $3 billion a year by not outsourcing many non-combat duties to the private sector."[16] He changed things literally overnight, and the costs to the American taxpayer soared.

Ultimately, private contractors outnumbered U.S. troops in Iraq. Contractors like KBR, a former Halliburton subsidiary, made billions in no-bid contracts (another anomaly in that free enterprise argument) despite findings of repeated misconduct, overcharging, fraud, kickbacks, and negligence in the deaths of American soldiers. One of my favorite examples was documented in a Pentagon report. In one contract, the DOD agreed to pay KBR $5 million a year to repair tactical vehicles at Joint Base Balad outside Baghdad. The military was billed for 144 civilian mechanics, each supposedly working 112.5 hours a month. In fact, each worker was logging about forty-three minutes of work a month, with virtually no oversight. Between late 2008 and mid-2009, KBR performed less than 7 percent of the work it was expected to do but still got paid in full. "The $4.6 million blown on this particular contract is a relatively small loss considering that in 2009 alone, the government had a blanket deal worth $5 billion with KBR. Just days before the Pentagon released the Balad report, KBR announced it had won a new $2.3 billion-plus, five-year Iraq contract."[17]

Blackwater Security, now known as XeServices LLC, behaved so outrageously that it was banned from Iraq. Under its new name, it is still going gangbusters in Afghanistan. To date, thanks to friends in high places, it has raked in more than a billion dollars in government contracts. At least 90 percent of its work comes through the government, and about two-thirds of those deals are acquired with no competitive bidding. To fully understand Blackwater's exploits, I recommend Jeremy Scahill's book on the company, *Blackwater: The Rise of the World's Most Powerful Mercenary Army.*

On January 14, 2010, Blackwater's founder, Erik Prince, delivered a speech at the University of Michigan, in which he discussed various secret operations and his plans for the company. Despite resigning as president and purportedly moving to Bahrain, he sounded as if he was still actively managing corporate affairs. He talked about "calling in multiple airstrikes" in Afghanistan, spoke with disdain about the Geneva Conventions, proposed that "the U.S. government deploy armed private contractors to fight 'terrorists' in Nigeria, Yemen, Somalia, and Saudi Arabia . . . and described his company's work in Pakistan, contradicting the official, public line that Blackwater is not in Pakistan."[18]

The biggest concerns with private contractors doing the work of our military are the lack of accountability, rogue missions, and questions of loyalty. Corporations now have a huge influence on our foreign policy and military operations. Company employees are responsible to their bosses, who are driven by the corporation's bottom line, share price, and stockholders. The United States is just another client. As we expand our military activity, we rely increasingly on these private "soldiers" to do the work.

We're not only contracting out our national security but we're turning existing government employees into private operatives. Our federal employees have always been able to moonlight in other jobs with appropriate approvals, but did you know this applies to the CIA? As with the argument companies make to justify huge CEO salaries, the agency says that allowing agents to do outside work keeps them from defecting to the private sector. Yet their "off-site" work includes delivering intelligence, directly or indirectly, to multinational corporations and hedge fund investors. We're training and informing agents so they can advise global decision-makers while still employed by U.S. intelligence agencies.

How about those private contractors who simply "lose" taxpayer money? From April 2003 to mid-2004, the United States

Federal Reserve shipped *$12 billion* in U.S. currency to Iraq. The U.S. military delivered the money to the Coalition Provisional Authority (CPA) for rebuilding efforts. At least $9 billion still is unaccounted for.

Investigative journalists Donald Barlett and James Steele delved into these events. "Accountable to no one, its finances 'off the books' for US government purposes, the CPA provided an unprecedented opportunity for fraud, waste, and corruption involving American government officials, American contractors, renegade Iraqis, and many others."[19] These reporters noted that many Washington insiders excuse wartime accounting irregularities. "But that doesn't explain why the Pentagon cuts checks for millions of dollars and mails them to anonymous post office boxes in tax havens. Nor does it explain the secrecy accorded its contractors. But it does help explain why the Pentagon is unable to reconcile more than $1 trillion in spending—*that's trillion, not billion.*" And according to National Journal's *Government Executive* magazine, "President Obama is on track to spend more on defense, in real dollars, than any other president has in one term of office since World War II."

For all of these reasons, Defense Secretary Robert M. Gates declared that reversing our military outsourcing is a major priority. He planned to hire thousands of civil servants to replace these contractors in the next several years. It is unknown whether his successor will follow this agenda. While this restructuring would increase the government payroll, it would decrease the overall cost to American taxpayers. More important, it would put decision-making, public accountability, and the control of information and personnel back where it belongs.

Another welcome policy shift was announced by President Obama in a speech to the graduating class at West Point on May 22, 2010. He rejected the Bush Doctrine in favor of international cooperation.

The burdens of this century cannot fall on our soldiers alone. It also cannot fall on American shoulders alone. Our adversaries would like to see America sap its strength by overextending our power. And in the past, we've always had the foresight to avoid acting alone. We were part of the most powerful wartime coalition in human history through World War II. We stitched together a community of free nations and institutions to endure and ultimately prevail during a Cold War.

Yes, we are clear-eyed about the shortfalls of our international system. But America has not succeeded by stepping out of the currents of cooperation—we have succeeded by steering those currents in the direction of liberty and justice, so nations thrive by meeting their responsibilities and face consequences when they don't.

Real patriots should support this turn of events. This policy was restated in March 2011 when President Obama delivered a national address on U.S. involvement in Libya. He reiterated that we were enforcing a no-fly zone according to the U.N. resolution and would not put troops on the ground. We'll see.

America must demand that other nations share the burden of maintaining global stability. As long as we carry the load, they are free to invest elsewhere—investments that make them stronger and more competitive in the long run. Right now, American taxpayers are subsidizing other nations' nonmilitary opportunities. If conflict threatens their stability and financial security, these countries will step up to the plate.

The national security policies and goals now in vogue are misguided and dangerous in other ways. America cannot use warfare to remake the world in its image. It can, however, remake itself into something the Founders would disown. In recent years, our leaders have used fear and misplaced nationalism to justify a crackdown on constitutional safeguards. But as Ben Franklin said, "Those who would give up liberty for security deserve neither liberty nor security."

In the throes of a disaster, we are at our best. Divisions evaporate and our true character shines. But that mood can change quickly, with devastating results for our liberties and fundamental values.

On 9/11, I was aboard an airplane at Newark waiting to fly to the West Coast. From my seat, I watched the first plane hit the towers on that clear September morning. In the days that followed, Old Glory adorned homes, car antennas, and clothing from Harlem to the East Village. Thousands of New Yorkers lined up to help clear rubble, search for survivors, give blood, feed rescuers—doing anything they could to help. In the aftermath, things turned ugly. Suddenly those without flag pins in their lapels were disloyal. Those who questioned military strategy were traitors. It is a test of true patriotism to defend simultaneously the nation and our democratic principles when both are under attack.

There are shameful moments throughout our history that should be required reading during such moments. John Adams had his Alien and Sedition Acts. Thomas Jefferson described that time as "a reign of witches." Woodrow Wilson used the Sedition Act of 1918 to prohibit "any disloyal, profane, scurrilous, or abusive language about the form of government of the United States ... or the flag of the United States, or the uniform of the Army or Navy."

The post–World War I "Red Scare" prompted U.S. Attorney General A. Mitchell Palmer to conduct raids and deport people who were expressing unpopular opinions. As is often the case, the mainstream press was caught up in the fever. The *Washington Post* endorsed Palmer's rash actions. "There is no time to waste on hairsplitting over infringement of liberties."[20] Yet one U.S. attorney, Francis Fisher Kane, resigned in protest. "We appear to be attempting to repress a political party. . . . By such methods we drive underground and make dangerous what was not dangerous before." In June 1920, Massachusetts District Court Judge George Anderson overturned several government deportations. He wrote that "a mob is a mob, whether made up of Government officials acting under instructions from the Department of Justice, or of criminals and loafers and the vicious classes." His ruling effectively ended the raids.[21]

By 1942, FDR was interning American citizens of Japanese descent. Japanese Americans were banned from the entire Pacific coast, except for those locked in the camps. Our Census Bureau helped out by providing confidential information to help locate those citizens. In 1988, President Reagan acknowledged that this action had been based on "race prejudice, war hysteria, and a failure of political leadership." And you wonder why Hispanic American legal residents are hesitant to fill out census forms?

The hunt for communists in the forties and fifties, the McCarthy era, reached such a fever pitch that thought itself became a crime, and entire segments of the population were ostracized as a result. Liberalism was tainted with this broad brush, and even today we see signs at protests accusing Democrats, even the president, of communist leanings. It would be laughable if the consequences of such idiocy were not so dire.

Looking back at the Cold War years, our concern, even fear, was understandable, yet our reactions and tactics were outrageous. Ultimately, cooler heads prevailed and members of both political parties took a stand against McCarthyism and its reactionary threat to our democracy.

With the benefit of hindsight, we wonder, how could they do those things? Yet today, when we get scared or angry, we're quick to follow suit. In threatening times, leaders make mistakes, but they also use our emotions to grab power and serve partisan interests.

A true patriot should always step back and remember what

protects long-term national interests: the Constitution and our democratic principles. Sometimes this requires faith that our system is strong enough to survive. Millions of Americans have died defending those values. We tell the world to adopt our ideals. We shouldn't be so quick to abandon them in challenging times.

This willingness to ditch the rule of law and hobble our liberties in the name of national security reemerged in our response to Islamic fundamentalism and the global war on terror. When frightened, many people see weakness rather than strength in our core values of openness, liberty, and the rule of law. Those who have faith in these principles are described as being soft on terror, as un-American, appeasers, or even traitors. People support the abridgements of our own freedoms out of fear, not patriotism.

In his 2010 West Point commencement address, President Obama emphasized that "al Qaeda and its affiliates are small men on the wrong side of history. They lead no nation. They lead no religion. We need not give in to fear every time a terrorist tries to scare us. We should not discard our freedoms because extremists try to exploit them . . . we will promote these values above all by living them—through our fidelity to the rule of law and our Constitution, even when it's hard; even when we're being attacked; even when we're in the midst of war."

His words ring true, but no action has followed. He has not relinquished the broad executive powers that President Bush assembled, and he supported the 2011 extension of the Patriot Act. Republicans object to his "overreaching," but they created the unitary presidency during his predecessor's administration. Invariably, people forget that the abusive power they grant to *their* side can end up in the hands of their opponents.

I believe in a strong military. I wouldn't hesitate to do all that is necessary to protect our country, and I understand that our strategic interests are wide-ranging. But it is not in America's interest to mortgage our future, in lives and money, to spread democracy at the end of a gun, regardless of the enormous corporate profits at stake. A full-scale military assault against individuals or small groups scattered across the globe does not serve our interests; in fact, it subverts them by breeding more trouble and miring us in ever-expanding conflict. Historically, intelligence gathering, covert activity, police actions, and diplomacy produce the best results in such circumstances. They must once again be our primary tools.

Finally, twenty-first-century threats require a major shift in our military policies, defense technologies, and concepts of national security. The entrenched interests will fight this in every possible way, and we must be particularly careful about the temptation to further invade citizen privacy and our civil liberties. Fears about cyberterrorism and the opportunities to hack into virtually every electronic communication make the balancing act both necessary and precarious.

In the aftermath of 9/11, signs appeared depicting our flag and the words, "These colors don't run." Bravery in the face of danger is a national characteristic I will always defend, but my America is not a country in search of a fight. We have always prided ourselves on being smart, not bellicose; on having the technology, the intelligence, and the international sway to get what we need without sacrificing our blood and treasure unless faced with no other alternative. Today, as deficits soar, we are cutting back on critical domestic programs, but thus far, the defense budget is quite secure. Until we recognize that our current strategies are not promoting national security, but are themselves a threat to our safety and freedom, we are riding a downward spiral from which we may not recover.

# Our Greatest Strengths

As America struggles to recover from the great recession of 2008, we must resist the urge to pull back from the open, diverse society that has made this nation so extraordinary. The current culture wars are inspiring rhetoric, policies, and legislation that seek to rewrite our founding principles. This is an inclusive society. We wrestle with our differences, moving slowly at times, and then, with sudden clarity, we accelerate toward Jefferson's goals of liberty, equality, and justice for all. As divisive as things seem now, a look back reminds us just how far we've come and what enormous benefits we have accrued by keeping faith with his vision. Today, our divisions seem insurmountable, but they are not. Americans have, with the Civil War as the one tragic exception, found peaceful ways to coexist, even as groups cherish their unique heritage, values, or practices.

As threatening as change can be, this nation has opened its doors to people across the globe who share our dream and seek only the opportunity to contribute and thrive. In turn, they have energized our society and refreshed the founding mission. They remember first the universal ideals and values that come alive in America and they will, in this land and abroad, pass on such dreams to other peoples and new generations.

Our Framers believed that all our children should have the opportunity to learn. Free, public education became a linchpin of the Republic. It is largely responsible for the broad middle class in America, one of the hallmarks of a strong democracy. In this age of knowledge, the foresight of men like Jefferson and Franklin cannot be denied.

Finally, good government—of, by, and for the people—is the core of our political system. By demonizing this institution rather than restoring integrity and rebalancing its role, we are hobbling what has, for generations, been a powerful ally of our citizens, our business community, and the world.

A diverse culture, our secure but open borders, affordable, meaningful public education, and a strong but restrained government have been the great strengths of this Republic, and if preserved, they will sustain this nation for many years to come.

# XI.

## *The Culture Wars*

The central conservative truth is that it is culture, not politics,
that determines the success of society. The central liberal truth
is that politics can change a culture and save it from itself.
　　　　　　　　　—*Senator Patrick Moynihan, March 2003*

A strong nation has cultural ties that shape its society for better or worse. Some countries are united by a common ancestry, others by a single faith. America was founded on universal values and principles. In 1776, the nation was rather homogeneous, but our Founders did something extraordinary. They imagined an ideal world and designed a political system to encourage its creation. Despite the existence of slavery and the inequities that women experienced, these men established a government that recognized certain inalienable rights for *all* human beings. We are all created equal with the same rights to life, liberty, and the pursuit of happiness.

Their words posed a daring challenge to future generations. Americans proudly embrace the dream, but applying it has been a continuing struggle. Our history is filled with battles, real and rhetorical, that forever altered society in the pursuit of this noble vision. Over time, these fights have extended our founding principles to a changing population, and by example, provided a democratic blueprint for people the world over.

Just as our national unity was challenged in the "Revolution of 1800" when Thomas Jefferson was elected, during the Civil War years, and in the tumultuous 1960s, we are again experiencing cultural and political disruptions that strain allegiance to our founding beliefs. We fear for our personal and national security. We worry that our children won't inherit the promised land of opportunity. We wrestle with our changing demographics; white citizens will soon be a minority in the Republic their ancestors established. The nature of family and marriage is in transition. In the face of such upheaval, can we remain true to a diverse and open democracy, or must we change to save the country?

With growing frequency, we hear calls to alter our constitutional system. Conservative leaders seek to repeal various constitutional amendments, restrict the Bill of Rights, and limit the statutory role of judges. In December 2010, Rep. Rob Bishop (R-UT) introduced a constitutional amendment that would allow two-thirds of the states to repeal any federal law. We're told that these measures will preserve the Republic, but in truth, they are meant to transform our system of government and national culture.

As you read this section, take a stand. Do you love America or just the *idea* of America? Some of the most revered democratic ideals prove to be the most infuriating in practice. Individual liberty requires commensurate freedom for those you may disapprove of. Real democracy means sharing power with political opponents, who, at times, may dominate the nation's agenda. The rule of law demands that justice be fairly administered to all citizens, even when a majority of people object to an outcome.

These constitutional principles are nonnegotiable. If you cannot support them, it does not mean you do not love America. You actually may have a better, more enlightened way to structure government or manage society. However, it means that you do not support the constitutional Republic that our Founders established.

While 85 percent of Americans profess some Christian faith, our government is not Christian; it is secular. "Secular" does not mean godless; it comes from the Latin, meaning "of the age," and refers to things that are not specifically religious in nature. If God is eternal, he exists outside human time. Man, on the other hand, must do a lot of rather mundane, day-to-day tasks—like governing. Jesus explained it rather nicely in Matthew 22:21. When asked if it was okay for Jews to pay taxes, his answer was, "Yes." He said, "Render unto Caesar the things which are Caesar's, and unto God the things that are God's."

Yet on May 10, 2010, Sarah Palin said, "Go back to what our founders and our founding documents meant—they're quite clear—that we would create law based on the God of the Bible and the ten commandments."[1] Her beliefs are shared by many religious conservatives, including members of the legal profession.

Let's examine this assertion. Most conservatives call for our judges to strictly construe the Constitution; to do otherwise would be judicial activism. Strict construction requires that, barring ambiguities, we look only to the document itself.

The Declaration of Independence, written thirteen years before our government was established, was the justification for revolution. It clearly describes the Founders' vision of a free, self-governing society, and uses the words *Laws of Nature* and *Nature's God* to recognize our inherent right to separate from England as free men. *Our Creator* endowed us with inalienable rights, including Life, Liberty, and the pursuit of Happiness. To secure these rights, governments are instituted among Men and derive their power not from the Bible but *from the consent of the governed.* The signers appeal "to *the Supreme Judge of the world* for the rectitude of our intentions," hoping that their decisions will be judged righteous and morally correct. Finally, they signed below the phrase: "And for the support of this Declaration, with a firm reliance on the protection of *Divine Providence*, we mutually pledge to each other our lives, our fortunes, and our sacred honor." While putting the fate of the country into the hands of the people, they put their personal fate in heavenly hands. There is no mention of religion, the Ten Commandments, or the God of the Bible.

In the Constitution—our *governing* document—religion is mentioned twice: The First Amendment establishes complete freedom of religion, all or none, for our citizens, and Article VI, paragraph 3 prohibits any religious test as a requirement to hold office or any position of public trust. There is no reference to the Bible, Jesus, Christianity, or the Scriptures.

If that is not enough, then let's go outside the founding documents and examine the *Federalist Papers*. Written by John Jay, Alexander Hamilton, and James Madison, these treatises explained every provision of the Constitution in hopes of rallying public support for ratification. The country was predominately Christian. Tying our government to the Bible might have been a strong selling point, yet Christianity is not mentioned a single time in the eighty-five famous essays. Following the passage in Virginia of Jefferson's Bill for Establishing Religious Freedom (1786), he reaffirmed the bill's intent: "To comprehend, within the mantle of its protection, the Jew and the Gentile, the Christian and the Mahometan." He wanted complete religious freedom for all, including the "pagans." George Washington himself helped Muslims "obtain proper relief" from a Virginia bill that would tax them to support Christian worship. The intent of our Founders was clear.

As for the Ten Commandments, they do not appear either. For argument's sake, let's see how they might affect governing in America. Here they are (in generally accepted wording and order):

1. I am the Lord your God; You shall have no other gods before me; You shall not make for yourself an idol.
2. You shall not make wrongful use of the name of your God.
3. Remember the Sabbath and keep it holy.
4. Honor your father and mother.
5. You shall not murder.
6. You shall not commit adultery.
7. You shall not steal.
8. You shall not bear false witness against your neighbor.
9. You shall not covet your neighbor's wife.
10. You shall not covet anything that belongs to your neighbor.

I'm not sure how Sarah Palin would handle the first two commandments without ditching our First Amendment regarding freedom of religion and speech. Number three is a real problem for American capitalism; no more shopping on Sunday. Number four, honoring your elders, is a universal belief, but does this mean no more retirement homes?

Finally, number five gives me something to govern with. "Don't murder" is a precept in all religions—even atheists support this one. But then it gets sticky. Various faiths debate whether the commandment should read "murder" or "kill." Some groups say capital punishment and war are exceptions—it's open to interpretation. Who decides when war is justified? What about the deaths of innocent civilians (as occurs repeatedly in the Old Testament)? Throughout history, Christian nations have fought each other—as did Americans in the Civil War. Lincoln lamented, "Both read the same Bible and pray to the same God, and each invokes His aid against the other."[2]

When we get to number six, adultery, I think a lot of people, particularly politicians, are going to filibuster. Number seven, no stealing, is also accepted the world over. Yet many biblical scholars said this actually meant no kidnapping—of other people's slaves. As for number eight, count me in, but without false witness, a lot of TV punditry and political campaigning will disappear. Nine and ten condemn covetousness. I agree. Commercialism has gone too far, but coveting drives our consumer economy.

Maybe we can find more to work with in the Bible. I'm not sure which edition we should use, but if it's the Old Testament, we'd all better run for the hills. The gay community will have lots of company as we stone adulterers, kill disrespectful children, change our accepted diet (no cloven-hoofed animals allowed), and abolish other freedoms enshrined in our Bill of Rights. If we turn to the New Testament and consult Jesus, a lot of capitalist principles will be discredited. Actually, capitalists, socialists, and communists can all make compelling arguments by cherry-picking the Scriptures.

The Founders understood this dilemma. Some were regular churchgoers; others were not. Most were affiliated with the Protestant sects, but among those who signed our Declaration of Independence were Anglicans, Presbyterians, Quakers, Catholics, Lutherans, and Unitarians. Some were Deists, others believed in a more personal God. They shared faith in a creator, but there were pronounced differences in their individual approaches to religion. Understanding persecution, they ensured that the government would not play favorites, nor would it mandate or suppress religious expression.

While they chose to establish a secular government, these men understood the important role that religion played in a free society. In countless letters, speeches, and debates, the Framers emphasized their belief that a shared ethical, moral framework is integral to a free, self-governing society. People who behave ethically and morally will encourage civil order. Our Founders knew that religion was an invaluable teacher (and enforcer) of such behavior. If people believe that God is watching and judging our conduct, there will be less need for secular rules and laws. The more citizens behave voluntarily, the freer they will be. The Framers *did not* establish a Christian government, but they did encourage a values-based culture; and yes, their references were Judeo-Christian principles.

The French writer Alexis de Tocqueville found plenty of religion when he came to America in the 1830s, but he noted, "You will hear morality preached, but of Dogma—not a word."[3] Thomas Jefferson famously created his own Bible. He took the New Testament and cut out the miracles, the Holy Trinity, and the Resurrection. When he finished snipping, he was left with his "wee little book" of forty-six pages, *The Life and Morals of Jesus of Nazareth*, in which "there will be found remaining the most sublime and benevolent code of morals which has ever been offered to man."

Those who worry that other belief systems may corrupt our values should take comfort knowing that the world's major religions and philosophies echo Judeo-Christian moral tenets. The Golden Rule is universal, from the Christians to the Hindus, Confucians, Muslims, Jews, and Taoists. Long before Jesus walked the earth, Confucious was delivering the message, "Love thy neighbor as thyself, and do unto others as you would have them do unto you." Mahatma Gandhi's seven deadly sins read as follows: Politics without principle, wealth without work, commerce without morality, pleasure without conscience, education without character, science without humanity, and worship without sacrifice. I don't imagine there is much disagreement with this list.

Hallelujah! I find this pretty encouraging. If these essential values are universal, does it matter which faith or personal belief system gets us there? The Founders didn't think so.

*A business man who is generous to all his employees*
*but falls in love with his stenographer is wicked;*
*another who bullies his employees but is faithful to his*
*wife is virtuous. This attitude is rank superstition,*
*and it is high time that it was got rid of.*
—Bertrand Russell

We get into trouble when particular groups try to enforce their unique proscriptions on others. In some faiths, it is a sin to drink or dance. In others, a lack of modesty is a punishable offense. However, these personal or religious mandates are not compatible with a free society. Every citizen is free to believe certain conduct is inherently bad; however, our legislatures and courts do not have constitutional authority to enforce those beliefs as law unless there is a neutral rationale. There are plenty of examples where political pressure or majority rule have compromised this secular principle, but over time, the system tends to correct these mistakes.

The constitutional ban on alcohol, followed by its repeal, was one such event. During Prohibition, politicians and judges succumbed to the temperance movement. But millions of Christians had no intention of relinquishing their gin; for them, taking a drink was not an immoral or unethical act. It was no threat to the cohesive self-governing society our Founders envisioned. Prohibition created a backlash of violence and corruption and criminalized the behavior of otherwise law-abiding citizens, and the Eighteenth Amendment was repealed by the Twenty-first Amendment in 1933.

Today, the government can punish irresponsible or dangerous conduct associated with alcohol, such as drunk driving. Laws against public intoxication vary widely from state to state and almost always require disruptive conduct or a threat to oneself or others before an arrest. (Not surprisingly, Nevada has no such law on the books.)

The criminalization of marijuana reenacts this old debate. Despite decades fighting the drug wars, millions of Americans use this drug just as others use alcohol. It has been the largest cash crop in at least a dozen states for many years. When listening to arguments opposing its legalization, simply substitute "alcohol" for "marijuana" and you will hear the very words that were exchanged almost one hundred years ago. Countless studies show that alcohol is a far more dangerous substance, yet because it is so thoroughly integrated into our economy and culture, no one would seriously propose criminalizing it again for adults. To tell a huge portion of the population that "our" vice is acceptable and "yours" is not is, ultimately, a losing proposition.

In the not-too-distant future, I predict this prohibition will disappear, and we will enforce for marijuana the same rules that apply to alcohol. In December 2010, Reverend Pat Robertson actually called for decriminalizing the possession of a few ounces of marijuana, saying that our laws were "costing us a fortune and ruining young people" who go to prison as nonviolent drug offenders but emerge as hardened criminals. This would seriously reduce the violent drug trade that has destabilized Mexico and is now terrorizing communities across the United States. We will look back with incredulity at the billions of dollars and millions of lives sacrificed to enforce a selective code of conduct. What most assures this course of action is the recent embrace of this well-established market by traditional capitalists who are already investing in major growing operations and distribution centers serving medical marijuana clients.

The battle over gay rights is no different. I understand the fervent belief by some that God has damned homosexuals, yet the laws in Leviticus also issue death sentences to adulterers and those who curse their parents or God. Actually, Jesus was charged with blasphemy for asserting he was the son of God. Leviticus provided one of the offenses which led to his crucifixion.

We hear arguments that tolerating homosexuality will degrade society; that our children will be infected or the institution of marriage will crumble. I won't argue about these subjective beliefs. Empirical evidence will not change religious dogma. However, the same arguments were used to keep women at home and to enforce segregation. Today, the president of the United States is biracial and we have our third female secretary of state.

Whether gay or straight, if someone's conduct threatens the health and safety of others, we have laws to address the problem. But the simple fact that one is gay, does not justify withholding protections afforded other citizens. Even if you believe homosexuality is a choice, that choice does not harm you in any way.

I understand how this issue is complicated when the prospect of marriage enters the picture. In 2008, California's Proposition 8, which restricted marriage to heterosexual couples, passed with 52 percent of the vote, but numerous Christian and Jewish leaders opposed this measure. There is no consensus within the Judeo-Christian community about this issue. Even former first lady Laura Bush has expressed her support for gay marriage.

The nation is struggling with our basic principles. While churches have the right to decide whether to perform religious ceremonies for gay couples, the civil government is bound by different standards. There are countless civil benefits that accompany the state of marriage, and such privileges cannot be withheld from a group without a neutral justification. The belief of a particular group, even a majority of citizens, that a person's status (race, creed, gender, or sexual orientation) is immoral, or that expanding the right to marriage will somehow endanger the traditional institution, is not a legitimate reason to deny rights afforded other Americans. This position was asserted by conservative attorney Ted Olson when he argued successfully to overturn Proposition 8 in California. This decision is now stayed while on appeal. Whether affirmed or reversed, this decision will not resolve the national debate. In the meantime, gay marriage has been legalized in six states and our nation's capital.

*Every* time we have extended basic rights, certain groups have prophesied the end of civilization as we know it. Read your history books. The battle is always the same: liberty versus order. Can a society accept these myriad human differences and still succeed? Absolutely—been there; done that. Tolerance reduces violence and increases peaceful coexistence, while mandating conformity means more rules, more authority, and less freedom.

The degradation of American culture is not due to a secular government, the alleged suppression of Christian values, or our multicultural population. It comes from our collective unwillingness to practice the values—integrity, civility, and responsibility—that our Founders knew were indispensable to a free and just society.

Philosopher Reinhold Niebuhr wrote about the notion of "group think."[4] "Self-preservation begets power, greed, pride—all those sins are justified in the name of the group. Even the most pious, religious or patriotic individuals may suddenly advocate war, torture, even the overthrow of the Constitution in the name of their righteous mission." Sure enough, we're hearing national politicians and pundits threatening armed insurrection to save the country from their opponents.

Our Founders had it exactly right. They may not have foreseen the extraordinary changes in American society, but their secular government was the perfect framework for such diversity. As Thomas Jefferson said, "Religion, as well as reason, confirms the soundness of those principles on which our government has been founded and its rights asserted."[5] But these men knew that this system would not last, that true freedom could not be sustained, unless our society *voluntarily* enforced these universal moral and ethical values.

Laws, both religious and secular, can be manipulated or ignored. Our system of checks and balances provides safeguards, but they can be circumvented. In 2008, the entire planet suffered a financial meltdown because of a widespread culture of corruption—in both political parties, in the regulatory agencies, on Wall Street, and yes, on Main Street. Rules and regulations be damned—let's all get rich! Responsible, ethical behavior was for suckers.

Remember Ben Franklin's words: "We must all hang together, or assuredly we shall all hang separately." We must unite in defense of the secular government our Founders established. We must acknowledge that our shared values are greater than our differences. As Americans, we must hold *all* leaders—in politics, business, religion, and society—to clearly universal standards of ethics and morality. Only then, when the Republic is secure, can every citizen rest assured that their personal beliefs and individual liberty are protected as well.

## XII.

## *The Changing Face of America*

Our nation was founded on certain ideals and principles of governance, not on someone's country of origin or chosen faith. We applaud our grand melting pot in civics class, yet, throughout our history, groups have attempted to define *real* Americans based on their race, ethnicity, and religion, not on shared philosophy. Today, we're cycling through another era wherein certain groups are inherently suspect based on these criteria.

Years ago, the Irish, Italians, and Jews were the primary targets of discrimination. African Americans were brought into the fold only after a civil war and acts of Congress. Lincoln, the Great Emancipator, wanted to send them back to their homelands but understood that this was a practical impossibility. The Japanese and Chinese had their turn. Now it is the Latinos and Third World immigrants, especially Muslims, who are accused of threatening American society.

Setting aside the issue of *illegal* immigration for a moment, let's look at the broader cultural debate sparked by our increasingly mixed society. While few people are overtly prejudiced, many white citizens believe America is being destroyed by its multicultural population. They argue that liberal naturalization policies, laws that protect foreign customs, and schools that expose students to other belief systems are diluting America's Judeo-Christian heritage and values. Practically, whites are losing the numbers game, and for many people, this is very frightening.

In 2010, more babies were born to minorities than to whites for the first time in the nation's history. Already, one in ten of the nation's counties has a minority population greater than 50 percent. Almost one in four communities have more minority children than white children, particularly in the red states.[1] Latinos now make up a majority of California's public school students, cracking the 50 percent barrier for the first time in the state's history.[2] On September 8, 2010, the Spanish-language TV station Univision won the previous week's highest network ratings among the coveted eighteen to forty-nine demographic. This was the first time the U.S. English-speaking networks were beaten in this key group of viewers. In Los Angeles and New York, Univision's local newscasts are routinely number one. Many of the top ten prime-time shows in those cities are in Spanish. National advertisers are clamoring to win over this burgeoning market.

If we built an impenetrable wall around this nation right now, deported all illegal immigrants, and *never* let another immigrant inside, Hispanics would still become the majority race in America within a few decades. By 2050, whites will be in the minority.

When we throw in the economic crisis and horrific unemployment numbers, no one should be surprised that tensions are reaching a fever pitch. But we cannot let fear dictate our response to this changing demography. For those who think they can stop the trend and thereby save the Republic, think again. Barring a coup d'état that dismantles the Constitution, shreds the Bill of Rights, and forcibly deports *legal* citizens, this shift is a mathematical certainty. For all those who reject such drastic remedies, what does this mean for America? Maybe, our very survival.

Most developed nations have aging populations; older people who are living longer outnumber the young ones. Germany, Italy, Japan, and Russia actually have a negative growth rate. This doesn't bode well for their economies or their futures. Our oldest baby boomers are now turning sixty-five. This will pose tremendous social and economic challenges for the country. But we're still growing—slowly, but we're growing. This is a good thing! Babies are a nation's future.

Yet, without immigration, we would be losing population. Conservatives might blame liberal influences, from contraception to women's rights, for the diminishing number of white Americans. It is true that education and access to birth control have reduced the size of families all over the world. So has modern medicine; we don't need to have a dozen children in the hope that a few will survive. Our industrial and technological revolutions increased productivity—fewer people were needed to man the farms or run our machines. The train and the automobile increased mobility, and smaller families could more easily pick up and move as opportunity or need required. I could go on, but suffice it to say, all of our major advancements have reduced the size of families. Even electricity, just keeping the lights on, reduces the rate of procreation!

Women are having fewer children, but their contributions to our economic and political lives are increasing. Here are a few recent statistics. Between 1997 and 2006, women-owned businesses grew at nearly twice the rate of all U.S. firms. They accounted for almost $2 trillion in annual sales and employed about 13 million people. Today, more women than men are graduating with professional and advanced degrees. The United States compares poorly with other nations in terms of women serving in national government, but our numbers are growing. These trends are not going to reverse.

Given this shift, you would think our politicians would support family-friendly policies that make it easier for couples to afford their children. How are we doing? Wages in this country have been stagnant or dropping for thirty years. Most lower- and middle-income households need both parents working just to make ends meet. We subsidize and give tax breaks to companies that export jobs, and Republicans refuse to reverse that practice. Union and labor policies that encourage living wages have been rejected. Family leave and child care policies are seen as liberal or socialist programs. The result is fewer kids and lots of credit card debt.

This country is a nation of immigrants. For generations, people have assimilated and contributed to the economic well-being of the country because they were given the tools to do so. We created a burgeoning middle class by providing a good and affordable public school system from elementary school through college. We built a manufacturing industry with jobs that could sustain a family on one income. We stressed entrepreneurship and opportunity, not a career earning minimum wage at McDonald's. We emphasized Adam Smith's economy, not the transnational capitalism that owns Washington, feeds off American consumerism, and hoards its jobs and profits overseas.

Once, we welcomed immigrants with talent and good skill sets. Students who came here to study were encouraged to stay, and we reaped the benefits. *Legal* immigrants gave us Google, eBay, Intel, and Yahoo. "Despite the fact that they constitute only 12% of the U.S. population, immigrants have started 52% of Silicon Valley's technology companies and contributed to more than 25% of our global patents. They make up 24% of the U.S. science and engineering workforce holding bachelor's degrees and 47% of science and engineering workers who have PhDs."[3]

Today, our doors are closing. When foreign students obtain degrees at our prestigious universities, most of them return home. Obviously, opportunities are increasing for them elsewhere, but instead of competing for these smart, innovative young people, we display attitudes and design policies that send them away. They may still work for U.S. corporations, but they do so in China or India. Why aren't we actively recruiting these people to come and stay, particularly when innovation and new domestic business are the only ways out of our economic hole?

On March 21, 2010, Tom Friedman wrote a column in the *New York Times* about Intel's Science Talent Search that honors the top math and science high school students in America. He noted that of the forty finalists that year, twenty-seven were from immigrant families, many of them from Asia. Pardon my stereotyping, but this group seems to respect serious education in a way many Americans do not. Being smart, studying hard, and achieving advanced degrees in demanding fields is a good thing. Yet, by the second or third generation, this emphasis has diminished. The offspring have become "real Americans."

The Canadians and Brits are figuring it out. They expedite immigration for multimillionaires who deposit large sums into domestic banks and for entrepreneurs who intend to create job-producing businesses in these countries. They target people with interests in such areas as health care and academia, and they actively recruit talented foreign students to become residents. Canada proudly admits less-skilled individuals to supplement the agricultural workforce. These policies are a rational response to national needs.[4] We should take note.

As for *illegal* immigration, just watch the movie *A Day without a Mexican*—a wry look at modern America without this labor supply. Before reacting emotionally to the debate, let's look at some facts that clarify the problem.

First, our economy would take a serious hit without this primarily Hispanic workforce. Americans look the other way when companies hire illegal immigrants (or undocumented workers) to do backbreaking work in the fields, in dangerous and dirty processing plants, in hotel kitchens, and in our own households. Corporations want cheap labor, particularly from people who can't complain about their working conditions. Americans love their low, low prices. Yet, conservatives scream when these "hidden" workers show up in the emergency rooms or try to send their kids to school, even when they've paid their taxes.

Yes, there is a net cost to the taxpayers for these workers, but why is that so? And is the added cost a necessary expense, or is it a drag on the economy? As I discussed in the chapter about corporations, here is another example of big business pushing its expenses onto consumers. Whether these immigrants are legal or not, they are unskilled workers who will earn minimal wages regardless of their status. They are likely to use social services even more if naturalized, because many impediments to access disappear. (This would be slightly offset by increased payments in taxes and to Social Security and Medicare; they might send less money to their home countries as well.) However, this would be true for anyone, legal or not, employed in these jobs. Sure enough, the Center for Immigration Studies reports that "the primary reason they create a fiscal deficit is their low education levels and resulting low incomes and tax payments, not their legal status or heavy use of most social services."[5] The alternatives are: Eliminate all unskilled minimum wage jobs, substantially raise salaries for these positions, or make corporations bear more of the cost of these workers. The final option would raise prices for goods and services that use unskilled labor, but it's one of those moments where "you can pay me now, or you can pay me later."

Americans pick up the tab for food stamps and emergency rooms either through our tax dollars or through higher prices in the marketplace. Some people suggest we should ignore their plight by cutting off access to public assistance. We should let corporations use these people and sell cheap products while simultaneously denying them schools, emergency medical care, and other basic necessities. Imagine what we'd be creating in our society—millions of ignorant, impoverished slaves (for lack of a better word), hiding from authorities and completely disconnected from American society. If you are worried about the criminal class among illegal immigrants now, just wait.

Illegal immigrants are doing difficult, often dangerous work that Americans will not do. In response to the charge that they are taking jobs from needy citizens, the United Farm Workers presented a challenge to Americans in 2010—*Take our jobs!* "Farm workers are ready to welcome citizens and legal residents who wish to replace them in the field. We will use our knowledge and staff to help connect the unemployed with farm employers. Just fill out the form to the right and continue to the request for job application." The job description reads as follows: "Job may include using hand tools such as knives, hoes, shovels, etc. Duties may include tilling the soil, transplanting, weeding, thinning, picking, cutting, sorting and packing of harvested produce. May set up and operate irrigation equip. Work is performed outside in all weather conditions (summertime 90-plus-degree weather) and is physically demanding, requiring workers to bend, stoop, lift, and carry up to fifty pounds on a regular basis." As I write, only seven people (including Steven Colbert) have applied. These workers are not taking jobs from Americans. Americans do not want them.

We have denigrated manual labor and depressed blue-collar wages. Maybe we are raising children with expectations that surpass reality. We tell them they should all attend college. We constantly tout the American Dream, complete with home, car, and flat-screen TV. Now, we're going to tell these kids they should line up to work in the fields and slaughterhouses?

For all the legitimate complaints about the social costs of illegal immigrants, economists will tell you they put enormous sums back in as consumers. The more impoverished you are, the more of your wages you spend on food, housing, and other immediate needs. Wealthier people save or invest a fair amount. Our consumer economy relies on people who spend most of their earnings. These workers do just that.

According to the nonpartisan Migration Policy Institute, an international group funded by corporations and foundations, "Immigrants are not competitive in many types of jobs, and hence are not direct substitutes for natives . . . [they] contribute to demand for goods and services that they consume, in turn increasing the demand for labor. And immigrants contribute to labor market efficiency and long-term economic growth."[6]

Finally, from a pragmatic standpoint, we do not have a system in place to deport 12 million individuals. Taxpayers do not want to fund the kind of Immigration and Naturalization Service (INS) necessary to track, process, and deport millions of people. The cost, magnitude, and invasive nature of such an effort would be horrendous.

Several industries, particularly agriculture, would be devastated if this occurred. Knowledge-based economies still need workers to harvest crops, clean hotels, hospitals, and restaurants, and work in dangerous manufacturing plants. It sounds callous, but we have people willing to do these difficult and thankless jobs for little reward. As our population ages, this need will increase.

Growing up in Texas, I worked with many illegal immigrants. The horse business was a prime employer, as were many of the farms and ranches in the state. I found that most of these people were conservative, family-oriented, and hardworking. They came to the United States in pursuit of the American Dream—for opportunity, not a handout. Unlike many natives, they will take the tough jobs and are grateful for a chance to better their lives.

Republicans are missing the boat with this group, as they are a natural political fit in many ways. While I do not support whole-sale amnesty, Ronald Reagan understood the opportunity and granted citizenship to millions of illegal residents while in office. George W. Bush pushed a reasonable immigration/guest worker policy (and was supported by John McCain at the time) but was derided as a turncoat by his own party. Even ultraconservative action hero Chuck Norris wants a rational policy: "I would give illegal immigrants already here a three-month grace period to apply for a temporary worker's visa . . . if they remained in good standing [for two years], they would be issued a permanent worker's visa. [A]fter an additional three years, they would qualify to apply for U.S. citizenship."[7]

CNN exit polls showed that 38 percent of Hispanic voters cast ballots for House Republican candidates in 2010—more than in 2006 (30 percent) and 2008 (29 percent). The Republicans elected two Hispanic governors, one senator, and five House members despite the controversy over the GOP's tough new immigration policies and fears of increased racial profiling.[8] Imagine what this party might do without the demonizing rhetoric from many of its members! Rather than saying illegal immigrants multiply like rats,[9] recommending they be hanged if convicted of a crime,[10] or suggesting that an electrified border fence could work on them as it does on livestock,[11] maybe a rational discussion of the problem is in order.

Securing the borders must be done *in conjunction with* a legitimate amnesty/guest worker program. To make immigration reform contingent on border security guarantees that nothing will be done. Like the war on terror, border security is a nebulous term. At what point do we decide the goal has been achieved? What is the measure for success? How much are we willing to spend on fences, surveillance, and personnel rather than funding a legitimate guest worker program at much less expense?

Thus far, fancy gadgetry (including cameras and wireless alarms) has not proven up to the task. We've contracted with the usual suspects, such as Halliburton and Brown and Root, to build such systems at huge expense. After tremendous cost overruns, we get something that doesn't work. Why not put some of our high-tech brainiacs to work on a solution? I'd bet more money on Steve Jobs than on all the establishment defense contractors put together. As for the wall, "Build it, and they will come." The illegals just climb over the fence, while the drug traffickers tunnel underneath it.

Much of the violence that is plaguing our border states and cities from Helena, Montana, to Atlanta, Georgia, stems from the drug trade, not the people crossing to work in the fields and factories. Mexico is turning into a narco-state and deserves the kind of attention we've focused on Middle Eastern terrorism. Well, maybe not. I don't want to invade our southern neighbors, but Governor Rick Perry of Texas has volunteered to send his Texas Rangers across the border to fight.

Beefing up international law enforcement, the DEA, and other appropriate agencies is critical, but we must not permit the use of our military to patrol inside our borders. The Posse Comitatus Act prohibits domestic military operations to protect *our* freedoms and prevent martial law. This act was seriously compromised during the Bush presidency with the passage of the National Defense Authorization Act in 2006. Expanding the use of federal troops on American soil sets a very dangerous precedent. Remember, power given under one president will surely be used by others—in ways you might find alarming.

We are a nation of immigrants. We are that glorious melting pot. Time and again, an influx of new citizens has invigorated our country—Europeans after World War II, Asians and Indians in the 1960s, and now Hispanics, Middle Easterners, Chinese, and more. This always presents a challenge, but it is an amazing source of energy, vitality, and enthusiasm, reminding us daily that America remains a beacon of hope for the world. We are not a staid or dying culture, but one that is constantly refreshed and renewed by those who believe in our dream.

We need these people to come: well-to-do investors, educated and innovative young people, and those willing to work hard in more humble pursuits. This human capital invigorates our economy. Reforming our policies to acknowledge reality is just common sense. Whether guest workers or naturalized citizens, these people should be tax-paying residents rather than members of an alienated underground economy. They should be schooled in the American Dream and in our system of government. Only through national immigration policies will we continue to grow our domestic economy, and only through inclusion and assimilation will we ensure that future generations cherish and retain our national values.

Our earliest political parties struggled with immigration issues when they had an entire continent yet to explore. But when pressed, the people chose inclusion. It is not surprising that today tensions are high, when our security and economy feel threatened and our long-standing demographics are changing. But remember, America is an ideal, a vision that survives only when conveyed to, shared by, and practiced with others.

# XIII.

## *Education*

For generations, our public schools were designed, at a minimum, to produce literate, civic-minded citizens who could participate in the political and economic life of the country. Knowing that an educated population was critical to a self-governing society, the Founders, particularly Benjamin Franklin and Thomas Jefferson, were adamant about expanding access to education. As Jefferson said, "Whenever the people are well-informed, they can be trusted with their own government."

Today, education is under familiar cultural pressures to conform to narrow standards and offend no sensibilities. Interest groups clamor to insert their agendas into the classroom. The Framers' vision is under attack by small groups of people who want to (literally) rewrite history. Our corporations are salivating at the prospect of turning this public system into a for-profit gold mine at a time when a knowledge economy is sweeping the world. The children we educate today will restore our nation to its rightful place as a global leader in science and technology, innovation and entrepreneurship, or they will oversee the last great days of a glorious experiment.

For centuries, only the world's clergy and elite could obtain an education, but in America, the opportunity to learn would be available to all. This innovation, the public school system, is largely responsible for the concept of upward mobility and the growth of our middle class. This is an essential ingredient in a strong democracy, but one that may be heading for extinction.

Throughout much of the twentieth century, a basic education was sufficient to qualify for a well-paid job. Our manufacturing industries were booming. People skilled in the trades—carpenters, plumbers, electricians—or those running a local business or restaurant were all members of a growing middle class. There was great pride in the work they did and the lives they led.

As America moved from the agricultural and industrial age into the technological age, our educational goals began to shift. What the country needed was more children who knew how to *think*. That may sound strange, but in a complex information-driven world, basic reading and math skills won't get you very far. Learning to reason—to analyze, research, question, articulate, debate, and extrapolate—is the essence of an educated mind.

Today we're entering a "knowledge-based" economy. All but the lowest-skilled positions require a greater ability to process and evaluate material than ever before. Computers and robots can do a lot of things, but so far, human capital is still the most valuable component of most businesses. Workers in a knowledge-based economy must be skilled in critical thinking and problem-solving. They must be able to communicate and collaborate within industries and around the world. Every major problem we face—energy, the environment, health care—will require serious brainpower to overcome. Innovation and creativity are the buzz words for the twenty-first century, and in this competitive global economy, America is lagging behind.

When reading about the dismal state of our elementary and secondary schools, I despair. We're spending more per capita on our students than any other country, yet over the last fifty years, test scores have been steadily dropping. We barely hit the global average for literacy rates. Our kids do well on an international scale in math and science until the fourth grade. From that point on, their rank-ing slips every year. By the time U.S. students graduate from high school, many Third World countries beat our scores. Our dropout rate is at an all-time high, as is the number of students needing ex-pensive remedial work when they get to college.

For those who blame our multicultural mix for these abysmal scores, think again. We're lagging behind other developed nations that struggle with the same language and assimilation problems in their schools. Often, the best students in our classrooms are first- and second-generation immigrants. They have been raised to be-lieve education is a privilege, and they are determined to make the most of it.

Yet, in our struggle to reform public education, we have com-pletely lost our way. In 2010, Indiana University professor Jona-than Plucker met with several leading Chinese educators. Asked to identify trends in American education, Plucker described our focus on standardized curriculum, rote memorization, and nation-alized testing. "After my answer was translated, they just started laughing out loud," Plucker says. "They said, 'You're racing toward our old model. But we're racing toward your model, as fast as we can.'"[1]

For years, Chinese students were drilled in the art of test-taking. Success on national standardized exams was the only measure of their abilities. Everyone—students, parents, teachers, and even local officials—focused on acing the College Entrance Exam. And what did the world say about the results? These people could rip off ideas from the West. They could produce cheap knock-offs. But they couldn't initiate or innovate.

Until recently, studies showed that Chinese college students scored high on test-taking but low on ability. "A study by McKinsey Quarterly found that 44 percent of the executives in Chinese com-panies reported that insufficient talent was the biggest barrier to their global ambitions. The explanation: a test-oriented educational environment."[2]

On December 7, 2010, these very same Chinese students shocked global educators when the International Student Assessment test results measuring fifteen-year-old students in math, reading, and science were released. "In math, the Shanghai students performed in a class by themselves, outperforming second-place Singapore, which has been seen as an educational superstar in recent years. The average math scores of American students put them below 30 other countries." Shanghai also took first place in reading and science; the United States scored seventeenth and twenty-third in these categories. This was the first time China was represented in the testing. Testing director Andreas Schleicher said, "The real significance of these results is that they refute the commonly held hypothesis that China just produces rote learning. Large fractions of these students demonstrate their ability to extrapolate from what they know and apply their knowledge very creatively in novel situations."[3] Of course, the students in Shanghai are not representative of all students in China—yet.

Despite the danger—an enlightened mind demands an open society—Chinese officials read the future, set new goals, and rallied the nation almost overnight. They abandoned regimented instruction and standardized testing in favor of a more liberalized Western education.

Can America get its mojo back? Do we still have the right stuff? Our national scrapbook is filled with remarkable moments, but in the last several decades, the entries have slowed considerably. Unless we ramp up our public education system and prepare children for twenty-first-century challenges, these pages could be empty in the years to come.

Yet, we seem hell-bent on turning back the clock. Not only are we standardizing instruction and testing, but we're turning our classrooms into a cultural battleground filled with aging warriors and antiquated quarrels.

Because of its economic clout in the scholastic publishing sector, decisions by the Texas State Board of Education influence the content of schoolbooks used throughout the United States. Social conservatives have dominated the Lone Star textbook committees for many years, but in 2010, their editing of American history generated serious controversy.

A majority of the panel decided that Thomas Jefferson's deism clouded his role as a Founding Father—so he was removed from the list of great philosophers that inspired our revolution, as was a discussion of political Enlightenment, in favor of a discussion of religious thinkers of that era. Momentous events, such as the struggle for civil rights, were glossed over while the rise of the conservative movement in American politics became more prominent. People from "foreign" cultures were removed or downplayed unless they fit nicely into the conversation these gatekeepers have constructed.

A board member for more than ten years, and for a time the committee chairman, Don McLeroy proclaimed, "I'm a dentist, not a historian." His Christian perspective "guides him in the current effort to adjust American-history textbooks to highlight the role of Christianity."[4]

Another member of the board, Cynthia Dunbar, is quite candid about her goals. "We as a nation were intended by God to be a light set on a hill to serve as a beacon of hope and Christian charity to a lost and dying world . . . the only accurate method of ascertaining the intent of the Founding Fathers at the time of our government's inception comes from a biblical worldview." She sees our public schools as "a battlefield for competing ideologies. . . . [W]ho will control [our children's] education and training is crucial to our success for reclaiming our nation."[5]

Despite her service on this board, Dunbar is no advocate of public education. Her children have been home-schooled or educated in private Christian schools. She describes "'the inappropriateness of a state-created, taxpayer-supported school system' and likens sending children to public school to 'throwing them into the enemy's flames, even as the children of Israel threw their children to Moloch.'"[6]

In 2009, conservative board members wanted creationism and intelligent design incorporated into the science curriculum. McLeroy says, "I consider myself a Christian fundamentalist . . . the earth was created in six days, as the book of Genesis has it, less than 10,000 years ago." In that debate, he was presented a statement supporting the validity of evolution signed by eight hundred scientists. McLeroy says proudly that he "[stood] up to the experts." Because of his adamant positions, he was removed as chairman, but he remains on the board.[7]

What are these people so afraid of? Most of them are products of a public education system that taught these "controversial" subjects. Sarah Palin's own father was a biology teacher who instructed her that humans evolved from apes. Despite this, she had no problem making her own decisions regarding faith and science.

During the Dark Ages, religious orders were the guardians of education. The liberated mind was a threat to their control. They opposed teaching the masses to read. They objected to the printing press. These developments meant that everyone could possess and peruse their own copies of sacred texts. Religious leaders were terrified that people might interpret these materials in ways the clergy disapproved of. Yet, as literacy increased and people began to think and debate, religion thrived.

The study of science does not erode religious beliefs. Christian fundamentalists are one of the few Christian groups that reject evolution. Most faiths have no problem reconciling science and God, as the former does not deny the latter.

I would never suggest that those who object to a science or history curriculum should be forced to learn such information. There are plenty of Christian schools that offer an alternative, and the home school movement is thriving. If the "agenda" in public schools has been so corrupted in the last fifty years, then why is there such a healthy conservative movement? Why do about 90 percent of Americans say they are Christians? There is no logic to the arguments other than Cynthia Dunbar's clear agenda—to win her ideological battle. She must have studied *1984*, George Orwell's primer on censorship and propaganda. "Who controls the past controls the future: who controls the present controls the past."[8]

Just as we are a nation of secular laws, our public education system cannot be structured to coincide with the demands of particular individuals or religious groups. As conservative Supreme Court jurist Antonin Scalia reminds us, "To make the individual's obligation to obey . . . a law contingent upon the law's coincidence with his religious beliefs [would permit] him, by virtue of his beliefs, to become a law unto himself." America would no longer have a rule of law for all citizens, but instead would have "multiple laws, each of which was tailored to the doctrines and commands of a particular faith."[9] Just as we do not apply Sharia law if a Muslim is on trial, we do not use biblical doctrine in lieu of U.S. laws when Christians go to court. The same reasoning holds true for America's *public* schools. Our education curriculum must not be designed to appease political or religious groups, but instead, it must truly educate our children to succeed in the twenty-first century.

What were the Founders studying back in their day? Their faith did not prohibit an expansive education. The Enlightenment was not a threat to their religious beliefs. The devil did not reside in the halls of higher learning.

While I would not hold today's students to the rigors imposed in President Adams's household, we can learn from his example. John

Adams was rarely home to oversee his children's education. In addition to duties around the farm, they were instructed by his wife, Abigail, and various tutors. When eighteen-year-old John Quincy left for Harvard College, Adams wrote this recommendation to the dean, with apologies for the deficiencies of home schooling:

> It is rare to find a youth possessed of so much knowledge. He has translated Virgil's Aeneid, Suetonius, the whole of Sallust, and Tacitus's Agricola, his Germany, and several books of his Annals, a great part of Horace, some of Ovid, and some of Caesar's commentaries, in writing, besides a number of Tully's orations. These he may show you; and although you will find the translations in many places inaccurate in point of style, as must be expected at his age, you will see abundant proof that it is impossible to make those translations without understanding his authors and their language very well.
>
> In Greek his progress has not been equal; yet he has studied morsels in Aristotle's Poetics, in Plutarch's Lives, and Lucian's Dialogues, the choice of Hercules, in Xenophon, and lately he has gone through several books in Homer's Iliad.
>
> In mathematics I hope he will pass muster. In the course of the last year, instead of playing cards like the fashionable world, I have spent my evenings with him. We went with some accuracy through the geometry in the Preceptor, the eight books of Simpson's Euclid in Latin, and compared it, problem by problem and theorem by theorem, with le père de Chales in French; we went through plane trigonometry and plain sailing, Fenning's Algebra, and the decimal fractions, arithmetical and geometrical proportions, and the conic sections in Ward's mathematics.[10]

Remember, this was an eighteen-year-old, not a university graduate student. What has happened in the last 243 years? How did we go from a society eager to challenge and expand its children's minds to one that advocates rote memorization in pursuit of a meaningless high school diploma? Why is the notion of an elite education ridiculed as liberal gibberish? Why is exposure to diverse ideas and opinions a threat to American values?

Teaching someone to think is the ultimate gift of liberty. With such freedom comes a bit of chaos. If we truly think, reason, examine, and question rather than digest and regurgitate, it can change our lives, our communities, and the world. That's how this nation was founded. There are bad ideas and good ones, but education teaches us how to discover the difference. Independent, educated people have driven innovation, exploration, and liberation throughout history.

I do not envy those attempting to reform our education system. The tenure system has to change. Administrators must be able to hire and retain good teachers and fire the bad ones, fairly and efficiently. Teachers must possess the requisite specialties for the subjects they teach; no more coaches teaching the math class. For years, Singapore, Finland, and Denmark have led the world in academic scores for two main reasons. They train and recruit teachers as true *knowledge* professionals, hiring only those who graduate in the top third of their university class. They also reject rote instruction and standardized testing, and, instead, teach their children to think! We should follow suit.

School infrastructure must be repaired and upgraded. Kids cannot go into crumbling buildings with bad plumbing. They cannot function without books and supplies. To our collective shame, this situation exists all over the country. While ritzy neighborhoods may have fancier digs and better teachers, there must be a baseline for all public schools below which none will fall.

We must abandon the liberal notion that every child can receive the same education, often in the same classroom, without lowering the bar for all students and, at times, costing the taxpayers enormous sums. In our quest to uphold the self-esteem of every child, many schools hesitate to establish advanced or remedial classrooms. Thus an entire group can only proceed at the pace of the slowest learner—a surefire way to destroy interest and enthusiasm for many kids.

Public school teachers cannot be all things to all people. When I was in K-12, teachers could discriminate (not inherently a bad word) for the good of the children. Kids with a higher aptitude for the books were put in honors classes. They needed more intellectual challenge and accelerated coursework to keep them engaged. Vocational classes and programs like Junior Achievement encouraged those who wanted a trade or imagined themselves budding entrepreneurs. Home economics was still popular for the young women who dreamed of marriage and a family. For some kids, athletics was the magnet that kept them focused on a good report card, and many kids participated in multiple categories.

Whatever their ultimate dream, every child was expected to learn the basics: reading, math, science, history, geography, and social studies. The arts were encouraged—drama, music, and more. Barring a doctor's slip, kids were expected to get a physical education as well—in the gym, on the track or ball field, and on the playground. Teachers understood the need to drain restless energy while teaching social skills and promoting a healthy lifestyle.

From time to time, kids were held back a grade. The idea of inflating scores to shuffle students along an assembly line would have been sacrilege. Self-esteem was important—everyone got an E for effort—but a blue ribbon, a good report card, or a high school diploma was earned; it meant something.

And the same was true for those who attended college. Acceptance by a university was a big deal. The competition was intense, and there was an expectation that entering freshmen were ready for rigorous college work. Today, universities, even prestigious ones, are spending enormous sums on remedial education for students who lack basic reading, writing, and comprehension skills.

It is not surprising that fewer than half of U.S. college students who first enrolled in a two- or four-year school in 2003–4 had obtained a degree by 2010. For those who initially enrolled at a two-year institution, only 12 percent obtained a degree and 46 percent had dropped out entirely.[11]

While achievement levels are dropping in our universities, costs are going through the roof. America's institutions of higher learning have long been the envy of the world, yet today former president Bill Clinton notes that "higher education institutions are pricing themselves into America's decline." On average, the cost of a bachelor's degree is up 50 percent since 1996, while an associate's degree has doubled in price at public and not-for-profit institutions. "The country is already on pace to be short 16 million college educated workers by 2025, and the constantly spiraling amount of debt that students have to incur to get a degree is going to make it that much harder to catch up."[12]

We need more good graduates, yet instead of building real universities, we create online diploma mills and construct prisons. Just ask California. Hey, one warehouse is as good as another. Or maybe we should turn the whole university concept into another business opportunity. Now there's a winner. Indeed, for-profit universities have become a booming industry in the last decade, thanks to deregulation by the Bush administration's Department of Education. Florida Republican governor Rick Scott wants to privatize the state's public schools under a similar model.

In 2002, the for-profit education industry got one of its chief lobbyists, Sally Stroup, appointed as Bush's assistant secretary of post-secondary education for the DOE. And guess what happened. "The industry embarked on 10 years of unrestricted massive growth thanks to expanded access to federal student loan money." Taxpayer money accounts for almost 90 percent of revenues at the big for-profits, but what do they do with all that tuition? "In fiscal 2009, Apollo, the largest company in the industry, received $1.1 billion [in] federally-funded student loans and grants. Of this amount, the company spent only $99 million on faculty compensation and instruction costs—that's 9 cents on every dollar . . . the rest went to marketing and paying the executives." [13]

These institutions troll for low-income students who are seeking a cheaper university education and qualify for Title IV loans and grants. Recent investigations conclude these schools are "'recruiting students with inflated promises, fudging financial-aid applications and leaving graduates with crushing debt and bleak job prospects'—and the borrowing at those institutions is astronomical." [14]

Does this sound familiar? It should. It is the subprime crisis all over again: deregulation, cheap rates, lowered lending standards to boost profits, government loan guarantees, and federal monitoring agencies run by industry lobbyists. What follows? Massive default rates as students drop out or give up juggling the debt. The annual dropout rates at three leading for-profit universities, Apollo, ESI, and COCO, are 50 to 100 percent. [15]

In the meantime, these companies and their CEOs are raking in the profits as they take students and taxpayers for a ride. If this is the future of education, we're doomed.

A good education is more than the key to our economic well-being. As the Founders understood, it is the key to a healthy democracy. Our nation's future depends on the next generation's ability to compete in a global economy. Our best hope for educating our children and preparing them to lead is to bring our public schools back up to the highest standards and provide the quality, secular education for all citizens that our Founders envisioned.

# XIV.

## *Good Government*

The question that we ask today is not whether our government
is too big or too small, but whether it works.
—*President Barack Obama, 2009 Inaugural Address*

For decades, Republicans have railed against Washington, saying that the federal government is oppresive and over-reaching. It overtaxes us, funds an incompetent, unwieldy bureaucracy, and is hurtling toward socialism. Capitalism is under siege and, according to the Tea Party, our very liberty depends upon a citizens' insurrection. Democrats describe a system that is skewed to benefit the rich, that ignores economic and political disparity, and that abdicates public duties to a powerful, unaccountable private elite. Independent voters swing back and forth, simply searching for honest, competent leadership.

Actually, Americans are schizophrenic about our government. When people are asked to cut various spending programs, studies find that a large majority of citizens, regardless of their politics, value most activities and are hesitant to reduce funds. Invariably they will target foreign aid, a sum that consumes less than 1 percent of the budget. Tea Partiers protest government socialism while carrying signs that read "Hands off our Medicare," and George W.

Bush was summarily dismissed by older Republicans when he tried to privatize Social Security.

When asked about taxes, everyone wants a break. Most people don't realize that 95 percent of the country got one in 2009. Even fewer know that Americans are experiencing the lowest rates since our income tax was instituted—excepting 1914–15 and 1988–91—and this during two wars, a major economic recession, and a burgeoning deficit. In fact, this is the first time in our history that we didn't raise taxes during a major war, with one exception, the war against Mexico in 1846–48. Essentially, we are conservative on taxes and progressive on spending—we want it all. Yet, most people express a willingness to pay more taxes *if* they believe the money is being put to good use.

On December 14, 2010, *Wall Street Journal* columnist Daniel Henniger asked: "Should the primary purpose of taxation be to support the government or maximize economic growth?" Note that he offered just two possible answers—the alleged liberal practice of spending our hard-earned money on a big, oppressive bureaucracy or his assuredly conservative policy of using these dollars to maximize economic growth. Henniger's conclusion? "To ensure American well-being, the pre-eminent purpose of a modern tax system should be to achieve the highest possible level of growth in the private economy with a competent, efficient state in a supporting role."

Here's the deal in a nutshell. From the outset, a broad reading of the Constitution gave Federalists the authority to initiate, subsidize, and expand economic growth. By "discovering" unenumerated powers in the Constitution, Hamilton established a banking system and created deficits to build early infrastructure and subsidize agricultural, industrial, and technological development. Big government and big business were a team.

But as the nation grew stronger, there were consequences. The concentration of wealth and power that Adam Smith warned about occurred. Individuals and small business owners were sucked into this vortex, sometimes riding a wave of prosperity and at other times plunging into poverty, with little control over these events. A social safety net and increased government regulations were created in response to the abuses that attend the growth of corporate capitalism.

Rather than an attempt to socialize America or suppress our growth, officials established rules to lessen the damage from such enormous private power. Before 1932, the fallout from regular boom and bust cycles devastated the general population. The Great Depression was of such magnitude that the Democratic Party, historically quite restrained in its use of federal power, established labor laws, a social safety net, and rules to encourage more honest competition in the marketplace. All of this was an attempt to ensure that unrestrained capitalism didn't destroy its seed corn—the workers and consumers it needed to make the system work.

The many regulatory agencies that protect the environment, monitor our food and drugs, or mandate safety measures across the business spectrum emerged to address dangers and abuses by big corporations. If we lived in the America that Adam Smith or Thomas Jefferson imagined, filled with individuals and small companies working and trading among themselves, we could dispense with much of this. A bad product would have limited effect. Localized pollution could be contained. An abusive employer could be chastised or shunned. Small, cohesive communities could care for those in need.

That is not our world. It never really was. Yet Reagan brought this frontier myth back to life in 1980. The three preceding decades had focused heavily on the American people—their health, security, and education. These policies created a broad middle class with good jobs and upward mobility. We were certainly having problems, as a new liberal elite experimented with welfare and poverty programs to change human behavior. Additionally, we were experiencing stagnation, inflation, and an energy crisis. People felt constrained and manipulated. They wanted new ideas, and Reagan's were dramatic.

Rather than tweak and rebalance our approaches, he was determined to jump-start America's economic engine by liberating the private sector from most government controls. He let go of the corporate reins and spurred our economy with subsidies, tax breaks, loose credit, and deregulation. Each time it stumbled or threatened to stray, our politicians, Republicans and Democrats alike, would beg and borrow to keep it happy. We didn't mind. With the wind in our hair and the world before us, Americans were having a hell of a ride. We couldn't imagine this beast might gobble our offerings, throw us off, and bolt for greener pastures.

In this global economy, the big players are no longer confined to their home turf. Technology allows them to operate anywhere. Investment and capital flow across borders with a single keystroke. Such countries as India and China have an educated workforce and fewer regulations. They are willing to pay a big price to get into the game.

So back to Daniel Henniger's conclusion that the number-one function of taxes is "to achieve the highest possible level of growth in the private economy." We've followed that maxim for thirty years and look where we are.

We've been over this in earlier chapters, but let me restate an empirical fact: tax cuts for the wealthy do not increase overall revenues or spur domestic business investment and job growth. Reagan's trickle-down economic theory has been repeatedly debunked by leading experts, including Reagan's own top economic advisors, Bruce Bartlett and David Stockman. The rich save most of this money, invest overseas, and buy trinkets.

Still a believer, George W. Bush cut taxes in 2001 and 2003 and reduced business regulations throughout his tenure, promising major economic growth. But the *Wall Street Journal* determined that Bush "shows the worst track record for job creation since the government began keeping records." The *Journal* credited him with 3 million jobs in his two terms, compared to the 23.1 million jobs created during the higher-tax years of Clinton's administration.[1]

Three months before Republicans pushed through the 2010 extension of Bush's tax cuts for upper income earners, the Congressional Budget Office reported that "the $100 billion in tax cuts on income above $250,000 would reduce unemployment in 2011 and 2012 by ... *somewhere between 0.1% and nothing at all.*"[2] Ignoring three decades of unequivocal economic results, Republicans still pitch their favorite theory.

Deregulation saves taxpayer funds that would otherwise go to such pesky agencies as the SEC, EPA, or FDA. In exchange, we get wonderful things like the current financial fiasco, deadly mining disasters, and offshore oil well catastrophes, not to mention tainted food and drugs, faulty consumer products, and toxic dumps. Again, the vast majority of regulations are enacted for a reason—because of abuses in the private economy. Contrary to Republican assertions, corporate America will not regulate itself—*it never has.* Any short-term economic growth spurred by deregulation is snatched back in spades—think savings and loans, Enron, Wall Street investment bankers, derivatives. The culprits keep most of their profits. The taxpayers suffer the consequences.

After an enormous taxpayer bailout, American banks and big companies are experiencing record profits and are sitting on billions in cash. What more do they want? A return to the Gilded Age, nothing less.

Small-business owners (the primary source of new job creation) tell us that taxes, regulations, and tight credit are not the big impediments to their expansion plans. What they need are consumers. They need people to demand their products. Even Wal-Mart blamed lower revenues in 2011 on the fact that customers couldn't afford to shop there. This means that American workers must have jobs—jobs that pay a living wage. At a bare minimum, such wages must cover housing, food, and health care costs. Assuming we want to maintain and improve our workforce, education costs should be included. To keep these people off the government dole, you'd better figure in some *guaranteed* retirement security (not dependent on Wall Street roulette). Now, if you want an American market for other goods and services, people must have a little disposable income.

The current Republican leadership doesn't understand or is willfully ignoring this other ingredient—supply *and* demand. Sellers need buyers. Buyers need money—actual income, not easy credit. When the broad middle class has good jobs and reasonable benefits, our economy does well, even when taxes on corporations and the wealthy are much higher.

Look, I'm a fan of low taxes, but they are not the key to economic growth. Even seemingly oppressive rates are offset by other factors. During one of the greatest growth periods this nation has ever experienced, Presidents Eisenhower and Kennedy presided over individual tax rates that peaked at 91 percent, yet the American economy grew at an average rate of 3.71 percent. The more equitable distribution of wealth (shades of socialism!) created a strong middle class, a consumer base that didn't need a fistful of credit cards. The rich got richer, but so did those on the other end of the economic scale. Some economists call this the "Golden Age of Capitalism."

Higher marginal tax rates provide resources for critical public investments that pave the way for private business expansion and job growth. They also encourage capital investment. Putting money back into a business rather than pocketing the proceeds creates a tax deduction and stimulates growth. As David Henninger says, this should be the goal of U.S. tax policy.

Through the Bush years, the top personal and corporate rate was 35 percent (actual rates are much lower once lawyers and accountants finish with the returns), yet the economy averaged a pathetic 1.71 percent growth rate and produced almost no new jobs. We are now experiencing the greatest disparity of wealth between the rich and poor in our nation's history. Yet, we're told to keep cutting the top rates, further weaken our regulatory agencies, ignore the public infrastructure, and shrink the social safety net that, for now, is keeping millions of people off the streets.

Here's a patriotic idea. Let's take a page from Alexander Hamilton's playbook! As the "father of American conservatism," his credentials are impeccable. He would be aghast at the way we've neglected his country. He would enlist the best and brightest not just to repair but to revolutionize our infrastructure.

He started us down this path when the nation had nothing, not even a line of credit, and built major infrastructure, created a banking system, and set us on the global stage as a force to be reckoned with. In the midst of the Civil War, Abraham Lincoln pressed Congress for money to begin construction on the first transcontinental railroad. He succeeded. That same year, federal grants were obtained to build agricultural colleges in every state.

And of course, there was FDR. In the worst of times, he started the Tennessee Valley Authority and brought electricity to the almost Third World Appalachian region. In 1935, he dedicated what is now known as Hoover Dam, a project that created four thousand jobs directly and many more in supporting industries.

In a little over two years, this great national work has accomplished much. We have helped mankind by the works themselves and, at the same time, we have created the necessary purchasing power to throw in the clutch to start the wheels of what we call private industry. . . . Money is put in circulation. Credit is expanded, and the financial and industrial mechanism of America is stimulated to more and more activity. Labor makes wealth. The use of materials makes wealth. To employ workers and materials when private employment has failed is to translate into great national possessions the energy that otherwise would be wasted.[3]

Since the early 1980s, the GOP has made shrinking the federal government a hallmark of every party platform. Never mind that the deficit and federal government have grown substantially whenever they run the show. Republicans are so vehemently anti-government that they bear no resemblance to the visionary can-do party Hamilton inspired, the party that was once the driving force that shaped America's future. It was the Democrats who thought small. In 1995, Newt Gingrich led the charge to abolish the Office of Technological Assessment as more government waste. He saved each of us ten cents a year. How times have changed.

The decades-long standoff between the parties in Washington has allowed our country's infrastructure to crumble around us. We cannot remain a global leader with a Third World infrastructure. In 2008, the American Society of Civil Engineers assessed the nation's roads, dams, hazardous waste systems, schools, and water and sewage systems. The country was awarded a D; we failed. Solid waste disposal received the only passing grade, a C-plus. It will cost $2.2 trillion to get the country back to a merely "adequate" rating in these areas.

The huge gas pipeline explosion in San Bruno, California, in 2010 was the latest evidence of the potential disasters looming across the country. As of 2009, the AP reported that Pennsylvania still had *wooden* gas lines in some areas![4] Our water lines are just as decrepit. Water is the new "oil," yet in the United States, our states are fighting over the precious resource as aging systems leak more than 6 trillion gallons *daily* due to disrepair. That's twenty gallons per person every day.

Dangerous, inefficient, and outdated—this is not the nation I grew up in or the one the Founders envisioned. Bridges, schools, the energy grid, and really scary items such as nuclear power plants crowd the list of neglected infrastructure. Because of the horrific nuclear disaster in Japan, politicians and reporters took a look at the U.S. nuclear situation, and the picture isn't pretty. While the Nuclear Regulatory Commission (NRC) has reported no abnormal occurrences to Congress in the past five years, the Union of Concerned Scientists "found 14 'near misses' at nuclear plants in 2010, and there were 56 serious violations from 2007 to 2011."[5]

In a congressional hearing on March 30, 2011, Gregory Jaczko, chairman of the NRC, and Peter Lyons, the acting assistant energy secretary, said that spent fuel rods would "continue to stack up outside American reactors in wet pools similar to two that failed in Japan's nuclear disaster, while the government and industry pursue recycling technologies expected to become viable by 2050 . . . cooling pools that were designed to be temporary and that filled to their original design capacity years ago." Senator Dianne Feinstein had this reaction to their testimony: "It is clear that we lack a comprehensive policy to manage the nuclear fuel."[6]

Sooner or later, politicians and taxpayers must spend the money to restore our crumbling nation. Right now, labor and materials are cheap. Workers and small businesses are desperate. Instead of handing out unemployment checks, or business tax breaks that are worthless without revenues, put people back to work creating our future.

Don't tell me we can't do this *right now*. Maybe Washington politicians aren't capable of managing the tasks, but there are plenty of Americans who could. I vote to put C. C. Myers in charge.

In the early-morning hours of April 29, 2007, a tanker truck explosion led to the collapse of a long stretch of I-80 near Oakland, California, a major commuter route into San Francisco. Government officials projected months for repair at a cost of up to $20 million. Officials gave nine construction companies one weekend to submit proposals and selected the lowest bidder that Monday. Here was the catch: Repairs had to be finished by June 29 or there would be a penalty of $200,000 a day. If the work was finished early, there was a $200,000-a-day bonus, up to $5 million, for beating the deadline.

C. C. Myers won the contract with a bid of $876,075. This sum covered only a third of C.C.'s costs, but he intended to earn the entire $5 million bonus. He finished work on May 24, just twenty-six days after the original accident. His bonus was less than a single day's economic losses for the state, estimated at $6 million a day, from the closed thoroughfare.

I love this guy. He got his union card as a teenager. Employers soon recognized his management skills and wooed him up the business ladder. As owner of his own company, he has earned a sterling reputation and plenty of money working construction miracles.

In 1994, he won the contract for emergency repairs on L.A.'s I-10, the world's busiest freeway. Transportation officials expected work would take twelve to eighteen months, but Governor Wilson said it had to be done in 140 days. Myers said he could work faster.

"Four hundred men and women worked around the clock. Payroll hit $1 million a week. When workers complained about the grueling pace, Myers offered bonuses, donated money to their kids' Little League teams, and handed out $30,000 worth of restaurant gift certificates. When he had trouble getting steel delivered from Texas, he hired a train—at a cost of $119,000—to haul it. Whatever it took. . . . He finished the job in 66 days," *two and a half months* ahead of schedule.[7]

Now that's my kind of entrepreneurial free enterprise system. There was open, transparent competition for the work. Tough penalties kicked in if the deadline was missed. Last time I googled Mr. Myers, his company had just received the 2010 Best of California Award of Merit for work on the Oakland Bay Bridge.

While America waits for the next infrastructure disaster, let's not forget that those private contractors in Iraq and Afghanistan are building like crazy—huge military bases and official compounds to house us for a very long time and a never-ending assignment to restore two countries. This last part is pretty cool if you're working for the government. Contractors build schools or hospitals, and then insurgents blow them up. It's Groundhog Day! Another government contract appears, and the work begins anew. Our elected officials have no problem with these appropriations despite the dismal outcomes and the usual trail of waste, fraud, cost overruns, deadly negligence, and outright criminal behavior. All this while our homeland falls apart.

Forget for a moment that, by now, we should be riding on high-speed trains and zipping alternative energy through a secure, automated, twenty-first-century power grid—that stuff is only for the Chinese. We can't seem to fix what we've got, much less create a new paradigm.

In one of our most critical gaffes, we have never created a national broadband system. According to FCC chair Julius Genachowski, "Broadband is already becoming the foundation for our economy and democracy . . . [and] will be our central platform for innovation in the 21st century." Today, we rank fifteenth among developed nations in broadband access and nineteenth in speed of delivery. Why? Because a handful of U.S. corporations see no reason to upgrade and expand coverage in areas they deem to be less profitable. They control the existing pipeline and would rather maximize profits by restricting content and increasing fees. Right now, they are seeking to charge people based on the amount of data sent and received and to censor what you can access. If your web provider wants to promote certain news or entertainment companies, soon you may have to pay extra for a competitor's material or accept limited and censored access. The WikiLeaks revelations will inspire even more attempts to restrict the Web.

Ignore those who argue that such government work is socialism. As with Hamilton's bridges and canals, Lincoln's railroads, and Eisenhower's interstate highway system, a public platform gives American entrepreneurs a chance to innovate and compete in an area now defended by a few corporate monopolies. And the original investors in this technology, the American taxpayers, would be guaranteed access to the information superhighway, regardless of wealth or location. These are the very things that should be taxpayer-funded and publicly owned and not controlled by private corporations.

In a recent study of 120 countries, researchers found that every 10 percent increase in broadband adoption increased a country's GDP by 1.3 percent. Yet the plan floating around Congress right now is to expand coverage to 90 percent of the nation by 2020. That's *ten years* from now. More than forty years ago, we put a man on the moon in less time.

The same is true for green energy. We should be using tax dollars to modernize our outdated energy grid to accommodate new sources of power. By mandating that a certain percentage of electricity be produced through alternative energy—solar, wind, geothermal, and biomass—the government can stimulate growth of a private market. Capitalism can then do its thing. Nope, this ain't socialism either.

From Hamilton's day to the present, our government has funded research and development, built the infrastructure, and subsidized early roll-outs to stimulate innovation and the rapid expansion of new technology. We used to know how to do this. "After the microchip was invented in 1958 by an engineer at Texas Instruments, 'the federal government bought virtually every microchip firms could produce.' NASA bought so many [microchips] that manufacturers were able to achieve huge improvements in the production process—so much so, in fact, that the price of the Apollo microchip fell from $1,000 per unit to between $20 and $30 per unit in the span of a couple years."[8] Surely, everyone can agree that this was a brilliant taxpayer investment, as was the Apollo manned mission to the moon, the Internet, GPS, the human genome project, MRIs, lasers, drones, countless drugs—the list goes on and on.

Government investments have been absolutely essential in creating major leaps in technology, leaps that put America at the forefront of scientific and business innovation. Private companies are not the proper vehicle for much of this work. They look for quick returns and easily marketable products. They rarely devote enormous resources to projects that may not pay off for years, even decades. If consumer acceptance of innovations requires major structural changes, such as charging stations for electric cars or a new energy grid for wind and solar power, corporations are hesitant to invest heavily without the government as a partner and early customer.

But there's hope yet. While the Chinese dominate the green energy markets, and Congress debates whether climate change is even real, one American group is moving full speed ahead.

The U.S. Navy and Marine Corps are converting to alternative energy to save lives and money. Fuel convoys are prime targets in wartime, and soldiers are regularly killed or wounded during transport. The cost of guarding and delivering gasoline pushes the price up to about four hundred dollars per gallon. By 2020, the Navy plans to use alternative energy sources for 50 percent of its energy needs—for ships, planes, vehicles, and shore installations. In the meantime, it launched a hybrid amphibious assault ship in October

2010. It saved $2 million in fuel on its first voyage from Mississippi to San Diego. Fighter jets are flying at Mach 1.7 on a 50-50 blend of jet and biofuel—but ethanol is not in the mix; it is not cost efficient.[9] Would someone tell Congress? (Last year's ethanol subsidy was $7.7 billion.) Let's hear it for the military. This is the impetus needed to begin our national energy transformation.

In November 2009, I spent two weeks in China meeting with political and business leaders. Everywhere I went, often traveling on those beautiful high-speed trains, discussions centered on green technology. That country intends to dominate global manufacturing, innovation, and application of these twenty-first-century fuels. It is currently the leading producer of wind turbines and solar materials and is among the top three in critical battery technology— all originally American innovations. And it is creating lots of jobs. "The Chinese Renewable Energy Industries Association reports that renewable energy jobs in China are increasing by 100,000 per year and reached 1.12 million in 2008."

Furthermore, "China has declared that 60 percent of its GDP will be related to science and technology within two decades." We used to lead in this category as well, many years ago. Starting in the Great Depression and for decades thereafter, we poured government funds into innovative research and infrastructure projects that provided the seed money and foundation for countless inventions and new systems. Both Jefferson and Hamilton would approve. By the 1950s, inspired by the Soviet threat and the Cold War, "The United States was spending 3 percent of GDP on research and development, which amounted to a majority of the total spending on science on the planet. Today, the government's share of overall R&D spending remains near its all-time low."[10]

Once the world leader in innovation, now the United States trails such places as Singapore, India, and China. A report by the Information Technology and Innovation Foundation examined national innovation over the past decade. Of the forty countries it examined, America finished last. Another study on innovation, by the Boston Consulting Group, found that America is "disadvantaged in several key areas, including *work force quality and economic, immigration, and infrastructure policies.*"

Please note those critical pillars of an innovative society: workforce quality (education and job training), immigration, economic policies, and infrastructure. How're we doing so far? I'd say a four-for-four wipeout.

There is much more we must do to compete in the global economy. But let's start by changing the conversation. Americans cannot see our government as anything but an invasive, incompetent, bloodsucking leech until our politicians end the generic rants proclaiming that the federal government is inherently bad. The same goes for taxes. But voters have been well-trained. Ring those bells and we start slobbering. There is good government and bad, just as there are good and bad taxes. Knowing the difference is key.

For all its flaws, our government provides some pretty good returns on the taxpayers' investments. Most of us breathe clean air and drink unpolluted water, thanks to the EPA. During my 2009 visit to China, I flew to Xian to see the magnificent terra cotta warriors, dating from 210 B.C. I thought I had landed in a dirty fishbowl. The statues are enclosed in huge hangars, and excavation has been halted until scientists can figure out how to protect them from the corrosive pollution. It was only a few decades ago that Los Angeles had a similar appearance. Rivers in Cleveland were literally on fire due to chemical dumping, and acid rain fell across the Northeast. How quickly we forget.

While the FDA needs to step up its game, we can be somewhat assured that most of our foods and drugs are not poisoned. Sanitation bureaucrats make sure our sewage is flushed away, stored, and properly treated. Other regulatory agencies protect our safety at home, at work, and while traveling on land, air, and sea. That mandatory auto insurance all drivers must purchase means you can cruise the roads confident that if someone hits you, they can pay the damages. Mandatory limits on work hours, discrimination laws, and safety regulations have dispensed with many of the abuses common to employees throughout our history.

The weather report you casually flip on in the morning comes to you thanks to the National Weather Service. It has gathered information from literally hundreds of thousands of reporting stations—just for you. If you checked the temperature on the Internet, then another tip of the hat to government programs that created the first computer networking systems and funded research that led to modern search engines and Web browsers.

The cops who keep you safe, the teachers at your public school, the firefighters ready to respond if that government-mandated smoke alarm goes off—all of these public servants are there to help you. If you lose your job when your employer moves overseas, have your savings in a failing bank, or face old age with few resources and no health care, don't fret; there is a government safety net to protect you.

The great capitalists should be thanking all these bureaucrats as well. Our market economy would not exist without government regulations and protections that allow it to function rather smoothly. The very freedoms it needs are created and protected by—you guessed it, the government. Our government has established laws that permit corporations to accumulate capital, own property, and limit liability, all necessary ingredients for their success. Our system of patents and copyrights, banking and commercial laws, and trade regulations all provide a very favorable playing field for big corporations in the economic game. This same government builds the infrastructure necessary to operate—our roads, schools, energy grid, and information highway. It educates most of the workers needed for these companies, provides critical research at taxpayers' expense for the private sector, and subsidizes countless corporate endeavors.

The U.S. Constitution is a rather pragmatic description of government operations. Many of them deal with the nation's economic well-being. Check out Article I, Section 8, which describes congressional powers. The government is charged with creating a stable money supply, regulating foreign trade, and promoting open dealings between our states. The section mandates enforcement of the rule of law that protects our businesses at home and abroad, and uses the tax code to stimulate business investment and expansion.

All those petty regulations that restrict certain activities actually protect American businesses from a corrupt marketplace. The government tries to ensure their customers and workers are safe, that competition is fair, and that certain transparency is respected so everyone can make reasoned decisions about commercial activities. Government has been critical to the establishment, expansion, and success of American capitalism the world over.

By establishing a safety net for its people, our government has recognized the inherent risks of a roiling capitalist system, and many programs now under attack were created to ease disruptions and maintain social stability. These very measures have protected rather than thwarted capitalism. As Fed chair Ben Bernanke tells us, "If we did not place some limits on the downside risks to individuals effected by economic change, the public at large might become less willing to accept the dynamism that is so essential to economic progress." More bluntly, the public bears a lot of the cost and much of the risk in today's corporatist system, while rewards are funneled primarily to those at the top. Without a safety net, social unrest could increase dramatically and threaten both our economic and political stability.

Don't imagine that our politicians haven't taken this scenario very seriously. In 2008, the U.S. Army War College concluded that "Pentagon resources and troops could be used should the *economic crisis* lead to civil unrest, resulting in protests against businesses and government or runs on beleaguered banks. 'Widespread civil violence inside the United States would force the defense establishment to reorient priorities in extremis to defend basic domestic order and human security.' The study says economic collapse, terrorism and loss of legal order are among possible domestic shocks that might require military action within the U.S." Bush was prepared.[11]

Our market economy relies heavily on a strong central government for many things: a secure financial system, valuable infrastructure, and early research into new technologies that later profit the private arena. The government uses tax dollars to reduce corporate damage to our health and safety. And those same revenues maintain social stability in an economic system that encourages tremendous risks for the entire population while channeling most rewards to an ever-narrowing group.

Both political parties must examine the demands they make on this institution—the Democrats expanding a permanent safety net well beyond the poor and unfortunate it was meant to cover while battling wars on poverty and other social ills, and the Republicans doing the same for farmers or corporations while mobilizing armies in the war on drugs or terror. As I've said throughout this book, conservatives and liberals may differ on the types of policies or programs, but they agree about the need for a strong central government.

We should always look at ways to streamline government at every level, but the current attacks are not productive; they serve neither our capitalist system nor the American people. Even if an action is constitutionally permissible, the fact that government can do something well doesn't mean it should. But there are many things that private businesses might tackle that should be handled by the government. And finally, there are things America desperately needs that simply will not get done without the government driving the train.

This government was created of, by, and for the people—not the business community, global partners, or favored elites. Those individuals who are given the honor of serving must understand that they represent human beings, American citizens, and realize that their duties include the defense of a transparent, inclusive system that seeks to balance interests, not enforce elite agendas or partisan beliefs.

The shared sense that money and power are the only currency in Washington must be corrected. This country cannot survive such a pervasive loss of faith. Unrest is escalating, and there may be more economic troubles yet to come. It is not time to dismantle our system of government but to redouble demands that it be strengthened in service of our nation and her citizens.

# XV.

## *Patriot Acts*

If we don't change our direction, we're likely to get where we're heading.

—*Chinese proverb*

The cure for the ailments of democracy is more democracy.

—*John Dewey*

Our system of government is a truly extraordinary institution. It was designed to accommodate the diverse opinions of a growing population. It ensured, through checks and balances, that no one political party or citizen majority could rewrite the rules and impose their beliefs on other Americans. For this reason, it has mattered less who is in power than what that person or party can do while holding the reins. But we have upended this balance in ways that threaten our very survival.

Our election process has been thoroughly corrupted. The representatives we send to Washington are no longer beholden to actual constituents in their districts and states. Instead, they rely on a tiny group, a powerful elite, for their campaign money, their careers, and their financial futures. Politicians appease their core political base with words, but once in office, they unite across party lines to cater to a single coalition.

As elder statesmen, John Adams and Thomas Jefferson exchanged long and intimate letters that reveal the heart of their struggle—and ours. "The same political parties which now agitate the U.S. have existed thro' all time [debating] whether the power of the people, or that of the [aristocracy] should prevail."[1]

Jefferson, the romantic idealist, believed that his America would spawn a society motivated by personal liberty, public justice, and civic participation. America's aristocracy would not be measured by money or birth but by virtue and talent. Lobbyists and wealthy special interests, the "pseudoaristocracy," would be corraled by the federal government.

Adams remained the cynical realist. He couldn't imagine that the "common" man and more aristocratic groups would ever share a national vision and principles of governance, much less share power. Jefferson's idealism would foment class struggle and individual frustration. The real world was a more brutish place, and Adams knew how the game was played. He believed that, over time, the wealthy and powerful would control American politics as they did across Europe. Our vast territory would scatter individuals and dilute their power while leaving Washington to the monied interests. Jefferson's play for more states' rights fit nicely into this scenario. Divide and conquer.

Thus far, Adams has won this argument. Our cherished founding documents gave rise to real conflict. We are virtual schizophrenics as we wrestle with the concepts of individual liberty, the nature and size of government, and the influence of special interests. Voters are distracted by class and cultural divisions, worried that the other guy's beliefs and freedoms are somehow a threat to the country. All the while, a powerful elite reaps the benefits from our elected officials. It is the unsupervised marriage of big government and corporate America that most endangers the Republic.

The remedy is to reject the divisive politics we're seeing today and return to founding principles—to James Madison's precarious but Grand Compromise. If either the idealists or the "aristocrats" take control, the game is over.

Bejamin Franklin's concern about the function of the Senate, its accountability, and the nature of its influence is more important today than when he raised the issue during the Constitutional Convention. Our nation is now composed of more than 300 million people who migrate from state to state. More than one-half the nation's population lives in just ten states, but they have only one-fifth of the votes in the Senate. This means that 12 percent of the U.S. population controls forty-one votes and can immobilize that chamber. Given the transient character of the population and the changing nature of individual states, it is hard to justify this imbalance. Rules of the Senate, such as the filibuster, must be reformed to encourage open debate and actual votes on the nation's business.

With the Supreme Court ruling in *Citizens United v. FEC*, there are no more impediments to a takeover of our political system by corporate interests. Corporations are not persons, and their interests rarely align with those of the people. Citizens of all political persuasions must defend our democracy against the wash of special interest money that buys our elections and directs our national policies. Whether through congressional legislation or a constitutional amendment, we must strip away this misplaced power.

Our Founding Fathers witnessed irate citizens scrabbling over political issues, partisan newspapers hurling outrageous allegations, and politicians abusing their powers, but they could not have imagined we would deliver control of our elections and our government to corporations. Every patriot, no matter your philosophy, should storm the barricades to retake our power. The very heart and soul of democracy hangs in the balance.

If Congress is unwilling or unable to restore governance to the American people, then we must demand a constitutional amendment that prohibits corporate contributions, period. Money will always buy influence and access, but let it come from individuals. Make these contributions transparent, so that each citizen can better judge political actions and vote accordingly.

We must demand the highest ethical conduct from our officials. This movement must sweep every powerful institution in the country, from politics to industry to our social and religious organizations. We must restore trust in the institutions that make up our national fabric. The Framers knew that without shared morals and ethics, a self-governing democracy would not be possible. Laws do not guarantee good conduct, particularly when the regulators ignore or tolerate abuse. But citizens have the power to denounce and reject those who violate our core values. We must put country before partisanship and profit.

We must recognize that our current economic system is damaging the American people and the nation. Politicians on both sides of the aisle are protecting their careers by kowtowing to multinational corporations. These companies export every advantage, from patents and research to resources and manufacturing. They hoard profits abroad while pressing their global agenda in Washington's corridors.

History shows that America was at her most powerful when we promoted the growth and well-being of a strong middle class. In the 1950s and 1960s, our tax dollars were used to build critical infrastructure, to strengthen our public schools, and to expand access to higher education. We welcomed the world's best and brightest and led in research and innovation. We manufactured essential products, ensuring good jobs for hardworking citizens.

Americans have tacitly accepted the arguments that by catering to the corporate elite we will share in their prosperity and that any abuses will be corrected in the marketplace. We accept cheap credit rather than a living wage. Our citizens have become merely consumers rather than valued contributors in the global economy. Our workers, families, and communities are simply fodder for corporations' risky behavior and pursuit of profits. Rather than ask huge corporations to admit and carry their real social and economic costs, we use our tax dollars to build a growing but necessary safety net for our citizens. Rules and regulations are needed to stem corporations' behavior. The big guys can bear this expense or buy their way out of trouble, while small companies and entrepreneurs struggle to comply. We sacrifice everything for higher corporate returns and a soaring stock market. We're giving away the store—for what?

We must rebalance this distorted equation. We must support the real engines of American capitalism—the entrepreneurs and small businesses that strengthen our domestic economy. We must restore our national infrastructure and build the research, education, and immigration systems that will seed twenty-first-century innovation here at home. And we must realize that neither the stock market nor the GDP reflect the well-being of our people and the homeland.

We must examine our notions of national security. Patriotism is much more than symbolic commitment to our remarkable troops. The Founders would be stunned by today's U.S. global military complex engaged in a perpetual state of war. Our citizens are sheltered from the hard choices. There is no draft. Congress doesn't declare war or raise taxes. Instead, we borrow money from China to pay the tab. Then, we stretch a volunteer force to the breaking point to combat terror, export democracy, or enhance strategic interests; the mission adapts to our political mood. We are no more secure, but transnational corporations and mercenary tribes are well fed.

For decades, Americans have been willingly seduced by divisive political rhetoric. There is so much that unites us. We should not wait for a national disaster like 9/11 to recognize our commitment to this great nation and the dreams we share for ourselves and our children.

It is time we demand substance instead of sound bites and facts rather than ideological fantasy. If given the truth, Americans will vote to restore public institutions and invest in our future. Stonewalling will be recognized as partisan manipulation rather than legitimate policy. We will insist that our representatives work together to chart this course and earn the right to lead in every election.

John Adams saw our glorious Republic through the eyes of a cynic. He believed that citizens would abdicate the difficult task of governing to a powerful elite. We would choose political suicide.

We are on the cliff. If we fall, willful ignorance, personal greed, and benign neglect will be the reasons. Our constitutional system gives us the power to deny this ending. Our hearts and minds give us the spirit and wisdom to choose another path. This nation will survive our decision, but the American Republic may not.

# NOTES

## I: What Sort of Government Have We?

1. Richard N. Rosenfeld, *American Aurora: A Democratic-Republican Returns* (New York: St. Martin's Press, 1997), 476.

## III: True American Capitalism

1. Max Farrand, ed., *The Records of the Federal Convention of 1787,* 4 vols. (New Haven, Conn.: 1937), 3:533–34.
2. George Will, *Restoration: Congress, Term Limits and the Recovery of Deliberative Democracy* (New York: Simon and Schuster, 1992).
3. President Abraham Lincoln letter to Colonel William F. Elkins, November 21, 1864, Archer H. Shaw, *The Lincoln Encyclopedia* (New York: MacMillan, 1950).

## IV: The Rise of the Corporation

1. Franklin D. Roosevelt, "Recommendations to the Congress to Curb Monopolies and the Concentration of Economic Power," April 29, 1938, in *The Public Papers and Addresses of Franklin D. Roosevelt,* ed. Samuel I. Rosenman, vol. 7 (New York: MacMillan, 1941), 305–15.

## VI: The Not-So-American Corporations

1. "The Real Price of Gasoline," International Center for Technology Assessment, www.icta.org, November 1998.
2. *Guardian,* March 2010.

3. Philip Mattera and Anna Purinton, "Shopping for Subsidies: How Wal-Mart Uses Taxpayer Money to Finance Its Never-Ending Growth," Good Jobs First national study, May 2004, www.GoodJobsFirst.org.

4. Fhar Miess, "Residents, activists and decision-makers battle RWE-AG over acquisition of Felton's water rights," The Alarm! Newspaper Collective, October 18, 2002.

5. Ethan Rome, "Health Care for America Now," Huffington Post, November 24, 2010.

6. AP, February 5, 2010.

7. Donald Barlett and James Steele, "Deadly Medicine," *Vanity Fair*, January 2011.

8. Ibid.

9. Ibid.

10. Ibid.

11. David Evans, Bloomberg News, March 21, 2010.

12. Jo Becker and Ron Nixon, "U.S. Enriches Companies Defying Its Policy on Iran," *New York Times*, March 6, 2010.

13. Charlie Savage, "Sex, Drug Use and Graft Cited in Interior Department," *New York Times*, September 11, 2008.

## VII: The Great Recession

1. Interview with Nathan Gardels, Huffington Post, September 16, 2008.

2. Richard Lambert, "Crashes, Bangs & Wallops," *Financial Times*, July 19, 2008.

3. "Greenspan Urges Congress to Fuel Growth of Derivatives," *New York Times*, February 11, 2000.

4. Paul Weisman, "Gensler helps lead the charge to expose OTC derivatives," *USA Today*, November 22, 2009.

5. PBS, *Frontline*, October 20, 2009.

6. Brian Pretti, "Davos and Goliath," FinancialSenseArchive.com, February 16, 2007.

7. Bank for International Settlements, 1H, 2006.

8. Charles Duhigg, "Pressured to Take More Risk, Fannie Reached Tipping Point," *New York Times*, October 5, 2008.

9. Jonathan R. Laing, "The Endgame Nears for Fannie and Freddie," *Barron's*, August 18, 2008.

10. Greg Robb, "Fed, Treasury defend bailout of Bear Stearns," Market watch.com, April 3, 2008.
11. Roger Lowenstein, "Who Needs Wall Street," *New York Times,* March 17, 2010.
12. Economic Club of New York on June 9, 2008.
13. Scott Patterson, "Mr. Buffett Goes to Bat for Goldman Sachs," *Wall Street Journal,* May 3, 2010.

### VIII: Mapping Our Economic Future

1. Ashley Halsey III, "Failing U.S. transportation system will imperil prosperity, report finds," *Washington Post,* October 4, 2010.
2. Ernest F. Hollings, "Against Jobs," EconomyInCrisis.org, January 7, 2010.

### IX: Health Care for Sale

1. OECD Health Data, OECD.org, 2010; Conference Board of Canada Health Care Report, www.conferenceboard.ca, May 2011.
2. Dr. Frank I. Luntz, *The Language of Healthcare,* 2009, http://think progress.org/health/2009/05/06/170766/luntz-memo/.
3. Mitt Romney, "Health Care for Everyone?," *Wall Street Journal,* April 11, 2006.
4. Center for Responsive Politics, opensecrets.org.
5. Alan Fram, "Big Pharma Wins Big With Health Care Reform Bill," *New York Times,* March 29, 2010.
6. Newt Gingrich and David Merritt, "Tackling costs of health care requires some huge changes," *Des Moines Register,* June 13, 2007.
7. Ibid.
8. Kathleen Stoll, "Hidden Health Tax: Americans Pay a Premium," *Families USA,* May 2009.
9. Sarah Axeen and Elizabeth Carpenter, "The Cost of Doing Nothing," *New America Foundation,* November 13, 2008, NewAmericaFoundation.net.
10. Parija Kavilanz, CNNMoney.com, August 10, 2009.
11. D. Mozaffarian, M. B. Kotam, A. Ashario, M. J. Stampfer, and W. C Willett, "Trans fatty acids and cardiovascular disease," *New England Journal of Medicine,* April 13, 2006.

12. Kaiser Daily Health Report, Kaisernetwork.org, November 11, 2008.

13. Sarah Boseley, "PROZAC, used by 40 m people, does not work say scientists," *Guardian*, February 21, 2008.

14. "Pipeline antipsychotic drugs to drive next market evolution," *Healthcare Finance News*, August 7, 2009.

15. Kate Kelland and Ben Hirschler, "Superbugs: When the Drugs Don't Work," Huffingtonpost.com, April 1, 2011.

16. Parija Kavilanz, CNNMoney.com, August 10, 2009.

17. Atul Gawande, "The cost conundrum," *New Yorker*, June 2, 2009.

18. Claudia Kalb, "'Death Panels' Revisited: Studies Show Seniors Seek End of Life 'Comfort Care,'" Newsweek.com blog, April 2, 2010.

19. "End-of-life care patterns shift for patients with heart failure in both US and Canada," JAMA and Archives Journals, October 13, 2010.

20. Geeta Anand, "The Henry Ford of Heart Surgery: In India, a Factory Model for Hospitals Is Cutting Costs and Yielding Profits," *Wall Street Journal*, November 25, 2009.

**x:   Keeping America Safe**

1. J. Anthony Holmes, "Where Are the Civilians," *Foreign Affairs*, January–February 2009.

2. Thomas Jefferson to William Wirt, 1811.

3. Scott Shane, "Tonkin Gulf Reports Cooked?," *New York Times*, October 31, 2005.

4. Patrick E. Tyler, "US Strategy Plan Calls for Insuring no Rivals Develop," *New York Times*, March 8, 1992.

5. Antiwar.com, August 24, 2001.

6. Charles Pope, "Cheney changed his view on Iraq," *Seattle Post-Intelligencer*, September 29, 2004.

7. J. McGowan, "Neoconservatism," in *American Liberalism: An Interpretation for Our Time* (Chapel Hill: University of North Carolina Press, 2007), 124–33.

8. Jay Tolson, "The New American Empire?," *U.S. News and World Report*, January 13, 2003.

9. Records of Treasury Secretary Paul O'Neill, in Ron Suskind *The Price of Loyalty* (New York: Simon & Schuster, 2004).

10. George Polk, *Violent Politics: A History of Insurgency, Terrorism and*

*Guerilla War, From the American Revolution to Iraq* (New York: Harper, 2007), 209.

11. Alexander DeLonde, Richard Dean Burns, and Fredrik Logevall, eds. *Encyclopedia of American Foreign Policy*, 2nd ed., vol. 1 (New York: Charles Scribner's Sons, 2001).

12. Paul Holtom and Lucie Bérand Sudreau, "Trends in International Arms Transfers," Stockholm International Peace Research Institute, 2010, sipri.org.

13. Jack A. Smith, "Look Out, Obama Seems to be Planning for a lot more War," *Asia Times*, May 8, 2010.

14. The top fifteen countries with the highest military expenditure for 2008, Stockholm International Peace Research Institute, sipri.org/databases.

15. David S. Broder, "The war recovery?," *Washington Post*, October 31, 2010.

16. Pratap Chatterjee, *Halliburton's Army: How a Well-Connected Texas Oil Company Revolutionized the Way America Makes War* (New York: Nation Books, 2009).

17. Adam Weinstein, "KBR Bills $5 Million For Mechanics Who Work 43 Minutes a Month," *Mother Jones*, March 25, 2010.

18. Jeremy Scahill, RebelReports.com, May 3, 2010.

19. Donald Barlett and James Steele, "Billions over Baghdad," *Vanity Fair*, October 2007.

20. "The Red Assassins," *Washington Post*, January 4, 1920.

21. Robert K. Murray, *Red Scare: A Study in National Hysteria, 1919–1920* (Minneapolis: University of Minnesota Press, 1955), 250–1.

## XI:  The Culture Wars

1. Sarah Palin on *The O'Reilly Factor*, May 10, 2010.

2. Lincoln's second inaugural address, March 4, 1865.

3. Alexis de Tocqueville, *Democracy in America*, Harvey C. Mansfield and Delba Winthrop, eds. (Chicago: University of Chicago Press, 2000).

4. Reinhold Niebuhr, *Moral Man and Immoral Society: A Study in Ethics and Politics* (Louisville, Kent.: Westminster John Knox Press, January 1, 2002).

5. Thomas Jefferson to P. H. Wendover, 1815. ME 14:283.

## XII: The Changing Face of America

1. AP, "Minority babies set to become majority in 2010," May 10, 2010.
2. Will Kane, "Latino kids now majority in state's public schools," *San Francisco Chronicle*, November 13, 2010.
3. Vivek Wadhwa, "Why Skilled Immigrants Are Leaving the U.S.," *Technology*, March 19, 2009.
4. James Boxell, "UK to relax immigration rules for the rich," *Financial Times*, November 23, 2010.
5. "The High Cost of Immigrant Labor," at www.cis.org/articles/2014/fiscal exec.
6. Will Somerville and Madeleine Sumption, *Immigration and the labour market: Theory, evidence and policy*, Equality and Human Rights Commission, March 2009 at www.migrationpolicy.org/pubs/Immigration-and-the Labour-Market.pdf.
7. Chuck Norris, "Our Founders' Illegal Immigration Solutions, Part 2," Human Events, May 25, 2010.
8. Rep. Lamar Smith (R-TX), "The GOP's other Election Day victory," *Washington Post*, November 27, 2010.
9. Tennessee State Representative Curry Todd, TN, House Fiscal Review Committee hearing, November 7, 2010.
10. Conservative Florida radio show host Joyce Kaufman, WFTL-AM 850, August 2007.
11. Rep. Steve King (R-IA), U.S. House of Representatives, Washington Hearing July 21, 2006.

## XIII: Education

1. Po Bronson and Ashley Marrymen, "The Creativity Crisis," *Newsweek*, July 10, 2010.
2. Yong Zhao, "High Test Scores, Low Ability," *New York Times*, December 2, 2010.
3. Sam Dillon, "Top Test Scores from Shanghai Stun Educators," *New York Times*, December 7, 2010.
4. Russell Shorto, "How Christian Were the Founders?," *New York Times*, February 14, 2010.
5. Ibid.

6. Ibid.

7. Ibid.

8. George Orwell, *1984*, Part 1, Chapter 3.

9. Scalia quoting *Reynolds v. United States*, 1878, CARDOZO School of Law Conference, October 2010.

10. *The Works of John Adams*, Charles Francis Adams ed. (New York: AMS Press, 1988), 532.

11. "Less Than Half Of College Students Attained Degrees in the Last 6 Years, New Study Shows," Huffington Post, December 3, 2010.

12. Pat Garofalo, "College Graduates In 2008 Borrowed 50 Percent More Than Graduates In 1996," Huffington Post, November 24, 2010.

13. Steve Eisman, "Subprime Goes to College," Ira Sohn Conference, May 26, 2010.

14. Pat Garofalo, "College Graduates In 2008 Borrowed 50 Percent More Than Graduates in 1996," Huffington Post, November 24, 2010.

15. Steve Eisman, "Subprime Goes to College," Ira Sohn Conference, May 26, 2010.

### xiv: Good Government

1. "Bush On Jobs: The Worst Track Record On Record," *Wall Street Journal*, January 9, 2009.

2. "How Much Do Upper-Income Tax Cuts Reduce Unemployment?," *Economist*, December 7, 2010, M.S., Democracy in America blog, http://www.economist.com/blogs/democracyinamerica/2010/12/tax_cut_deal.

3. Franklin Roosevelt, speech at Dedication of Boulder Dam, September 30, 1935, in *Franklin D. Roosevelt & Conservation, 1911–1945*, 2 vols., Edgar B. Nixon, ed., (New York: FDR Library, 1957).

4. Garance Burke and Jason Dearen, "Aging Gas Pipe at Risk of Explosion Across US," AP, September 13, 2010.

5. Pierre Thomas, Jack Cloherty, and Andrew Dubbs, "Records Show 56 Safety Violations at U.S. Nuclear Power Plants in Past 4 Years," ABC News.com, March 29, 2011.

6. Jeff MacMahon, "U.S. Nuclear Fuel Rods to Sit in Pools—Like Those That Failed in Japan—until 2050," Forbes.com, March 30, 2011.

7. Chuck Squatriglia, "A Gutsy Guy's Big Gamble on the Maze," SFGate .com, May 13, 2007.

8. Fareed Zakaria, "Is America Losing Its Mojo?," *Newsweek*, November 14, 2009.

9. Thomas Friedman, "The U.S.S. Prius," *New York Times*, November 18, 2010.

10. Fareed Zakaria, "Is America Losing Its Mojo?," *Newsweek*, November 14, 2009.

11. Mike Sunnucks, "Ariz. Police Say They Are Prepared as War College Warns Military Must Prep for Unrest; IMF Warns of Economic Riots," PhoenixBusinessJournal.com, December 17, 2008.

**xv:   Patriot Acts**

1. Joseph Ellis, *American Sphinx: The Character of Thomas Jefferson* (New York: Alfred A. Knopf, 1997), 248.

# ACKNOWLEDGMENTS

My deepest gratitude to all those who helped on this project: Anthony Ziccardi, my editor, Abby Zidle, and the great staff at Simon & Schuster who were so patient and trusting throughout this process; Kate Malloy and Elizabeth Dewberry for their excellent critiques; Lauren Sasser for her research assistance; and my wonderful friend and agent, Jan Miller. Love and thanks to my wonderful friends who forgave missed appointments, rescheduled dinners and, when we did get together, my constant rants about the issues covered in this book.

And, to my gang: Sam, Abbey, Sadie, Cody, Bella, and Chick, who can always restore my inherent idealism when it wavers.

# INDEX

Printed in the United States
By Bookmasters